The History of Medicine

Other titles in the World History Series

The Age of Feudalism

Ancient Egypt

Ancient India

Auschwitz

Aztec Civilization

The Black Death

China Since World War II

French Revolution

Genghis Khan and the Mongol Empire

The History of Television

Influenza Pandemics

The Information Revolution

The Inquisition

The Islamic Empire

Israeli-Palestinian Conflict

The Medieval Crusades

Maya Civilization

Piracy of the High Seas

Polar Explorations

The Red Scare

The Rwandan Genocide

The Scientific Revolution

Transatlantic Slave Trade

Vietnam War

The Vikings

World War I

The Women's Movement

The History of Medicine

Lizabeth Hardman

LUCENT BOOKS

A part of Gale, Cengage Learning

GALE
CENGAGE Learning·

Detroit • New York • San Francisco • New Haven, Conn • Waterville, Maine • London

LIBRARY OF CONGRESS CATALOGING-IN-PUBLICATION DATA

Hardman, Lizabeth.
  The history of medicine / by Lizabeth Hardman.
     p. cm. -- (World history)
  Summary: "Each book in the comprehensive World History Series offers a clearly written and visually enhanced overview of an important historical event or period. The series itself contains many unique and interesting features, including a wide range of primary and secondary source quotations that richly supplement the fascinating narratives in each volume. The quotations range from unusual anecdotes to farsighted cultural perspectives and are drawn from historical witnesses both past and present. Most important of all, the World History Series is designed both to acquaint readers with the basics of history and to make them aware that their lives and their own historical era are an intimate part of the ongoing human saga"-- Provided by publisher.
  Includes bibliographical references and index.
  ISBN 978-1-4205-0671-6 (hardback)
  1. Medicine--History--Juvenile literature. I. Title.
  R133.5.H365 2011
  610.9--dc23

                                                      2011042000

Lucent Books
27500 Drake Rd.
Farmington Hills, MI 48331

ISBN-13: 978-1-4205-0671-6
ISBN-10: 1-4205-0671-4

Printed in the United States of America
1 2 3 4 5 6 7 16 14 13 12

Contents

Foreword   6

Important Dates in the History of Medicine   8

Introduction:
From Shaman to Surgeon   10

Chapter One:
The Beginning: Primitive and Ancient Medicine   14

Chapter Two:
Greek and Roman Medicine   29

Chapter Three:
Medicine in the Middle Ages   43

Chapter Four:
Medical Awakening: The Renaissance   59

Chapter Five:
Medical Revolution in the Age of Reason   76

Chapter Six:
Challenges in the Twentieth Century and Beyond   92

Notes   108

Glossary   111

For More Information   113

Index   114

Picture Credits   119

About the Author   120

Foreword

Each year, on the first day of school, nearly every history teacher faces the task of explaining why his or her students should study history. Many reasons have been given. One is that lessons exist in the past from which contemporary society can benefit and learn. Another is that exploration of the past allows us to see the origins of our customs, ideas, and institutions. Concepts such as democracy, ethnic conflict, or even things as trivial as fashion or mores, have historical roots.

Reasons such as these impress few students, however. If anything, these explanations seem remote and dull to young minds. Yet history is anything but dull. And therein lies what is perhaps the most compelling reason for studying history: History is filled with great stories. The classic themes of literature and drama—love and sacrifice, hatred and revenge, injustice and betrayal, adversity and triumph—fill the pages of history books, feeding the imagination as well as any of the great works of fiction do.

The story of the Children's Crusade, for example, is one of the most tragic in history. In 1212 Crusader fever hit Europe. A call went out from the pope that all good Christians should journey to Jerusalem to drive out the hated Muslims and return the city to Christian control. Heeding the call, thousands of children made the journey. Parents bravely allowed many children to go, and entire communities were inspired by the faith of these small Crusaders. Unfortunately, many boarded ships that were captained by slave traders, who enthusiastically sold the children into slavery as soon as they arrived at their destination. Thousands died from disease, exposure, and starvation on the long march across Europe to the Mediterranean Sea. Others perished at sea.

Another story, from a modern and more familiar place, offers a soul-wrenching view of personal humiliation but also the ability to rise above it. Hatsuye Egami was one of 110,000 Japanese Americans sent to internment camps during World War II. "Since yesterday we Japanese have ceased to be human beings," he wrote in his diary. "We are numbers. We are no longer Egamis, but the number 23324. A tag with that number is on every trunk, suitcase and bag. Tags, also, on our breasts." Despite such dehumanizing treatment, most internees worked hard to control their bitterness. They created workable communities inside the camps and demonstrated again and again their loyalty as Americans.

These are but two of the many stories from history that can be found in the pages of the Lucent Books World History series. All World History titles rely on sound research and verifiable evidence, and all give students a clear sense of time, place, and chronology through maps and timelines as well as text.

All titles include a wide range of authoritative perspectives that demonstrate the complexity of historical interpretation and sharpen the reader's critical thinking skills. Formally documented quotations and annotated bibliographies enable students to locate and evaluate sources, often instantaneously via the Internet, and serve as valuable tools for further research and debate.

Finally, Lucent's World History titles present rousing good stories, featuring vivid primary source quotations drawn from unique, sometimes obscure sources such as diaries, public records, and contemporary chronicles. In this way, the voices of participants and witnesses as well as important biographers and historians bring the study of history to life. As we are caught up in the lives of others, we are reminded that we too are characters in the ongoing human saga, and we are better prepared for our own roles.

Important Dates in the

2600 B.C.
The Egyptian Imhotep describes the diagnosis and treatment of approximately two hundred diseases.

460 B.C.
Birth of Hippocrates, the father of medicine.

130 B.C.
Birth of Galen.

1334
Bubonic plague, the Black Death, begins its sweep across the world, killing tens of millions.

2600 B.C.	460 B.C.	130 B.C.	1000	1100	1200	1300	1400	1500	1600

1543
Andreas Vesalius publishes his discoveries in human anatomy. Nicolaus Copernicus shows that the sun, not the earth, is the center of the solar system.

1590
Invention of the microscope.

1010
Persian physician Avicenna writes the *Canon of Medicine*.

1628
William Harvey publishes his findings on the circulation of blood.

1683
Antoni van Leeuwenhoek uses a microscope to observe bacteria for the first time.

History of Medicine

1796
Edward Jenner develops a vaccine for smallpox.

1816
René Laënnec invents the stethoscope.

1842
William Clark and Crawford Long use ether as an anesthetic.

1870
Robert Koch and Louis Pasteur develop the germ theory of disease.

1895
Wilhelm Röntgen discovers X-rays.

1918
A new strain of influenza, nicknamed the "Spanish Flu," kills between 50 million and 100 million people worldwide.

1700	1750	1800	1850	1900	1950	2000

1922
Insulin is used to treat diabetes.

1928
Sir Alexander Fleming develops the antibiotic penicillin.

1967
Christiaan Barnard performs the first successful heart transplant.

1955
Jonas Salk develops a vaccine for polio.

1980
The World Health Organization declares smallpox to be eradicated.

1983
HIV, the virus that causes AIDS, is identified.

2006
A vaccine to prevent cervical cancer is developed.

From Shaman to Surgeon

The history of medicine is the story of humankind itself. Throughout the ages all human societies, even those that existed before recorded history, have struggled to explain the phenomena of life, illness, and death. Healers and medicine men, priests and priestesses, shamans and witch doctors, philosophers and seers, modern doctors and nurses—all have tried to answer the questions of how and why people get sick and die.

With no understanding of the true causes of illness and faced with diseases that often did not even have names, the struggle to relieve suffering and cure diseases must have been greatly frustrating for ancient healers. The people of the ancient Middle East and Europe —the Mesopotamians, Egyptians, Greeks, and Romans—all developed ideas about illness and death, mostly relying on religious or theoretical explanations, and had well-established methods of medical and surgical treatment for a multitude of health problems. The humoral theory of Hippocrates and Galen guided medical thought for over a millennium.

The early Middle Ages, from around A.D. 400 to around 1200, was a time of stagnation in medical knowledge, with progress being especially slow in medieval Europe. The notable exception was the Islamic world, in which physicians such as Ibn Sina (known as Avicenna in the West), Razi (called Rhazes in the West), and Ibn Rushd (whose Western name is Averroës) preserved the classical writings of the Greeks and made great strides in medical understanding, especially in the areas of surgery, mental health, and hospital care. After around 1200 Europe began to experience a revival in medical learning, and universities with prestigious medical schools appeared. Despite this revival, physicians were still unable to cope with the catastrophic fourteenth-century epidemic of bubonic plague known as the Black Death.

The Renaissance (1400–1700) was a time of rapid expansion of knowledge in many areas, especially art, mathematics, world exploration, and science, including medical science. Men such as Leonardo da Vinci and Andreas Vesalius contributed to the study of human anatomy. The invention of the microscope provided information about the structure of internal organs and about microscopic organisms. The exploration of new lands brought new sources of medicines but also helped spread European diseases to the populations of the New World. Medical specialties such as surgery, mental health, and care of women and children made great progress during the Renaissance.

The late 1700s and 1800s brought a profound change in the way people lived. The Industrial Revolution was a time of innovation in machines and labor-saving devices, as well as the mass production of goods. The populations of many countries, especially in Europe and North America, moved from mostly rural farming communities into more industrial, factory-based cities. Overcrowded cities led to rampant disease and more attention to public health. Continued advances in medicine, such as the discovery of germs and the development of vaccines, led to the final abandonment of the old humoral theory. The development of antisepsis, which inhibit the growth of disease-carrying microorganisms, and effective anesthetics revolu-

tionized surgery. The invention of the stethoscope provided a new way to learn about the inner workings of the body. Medicine became more specialized, with specific bodies of knowledge in mental health, pediatrics, obstetrics, orthopedics, radiology, pathology, and dentistry.

During the Renaissance, advances were made in the understanding of human anatomy. Leonardo da Vinci, Andreas Vesalius, and Gregor Reisch (in his book Margarita Philosophica) *all produced detailed studies of the body.*

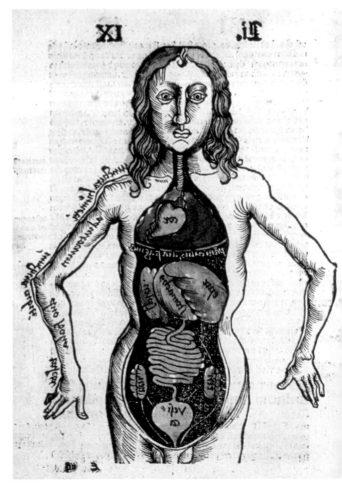

The twentieth century saw a continued explosion in scientific and technological innovation, much of it with applications in medicine. Antibiotics, the discovery of viruses, new cancer treatments, new classes of drugs, diagnostic methods such as computerized axial tomography (CAT) scans and magnetic resonance imaging (MRIs), artificial hearts, organ transplants, stem cell therapy, lasers, and many more discoveries have improved and will continue to improve the health of people now and in the future.

Life Expectancies Through the Ages

In his classic work, the *Great Canon of Medicine*, written around 2600 B.C., the legendary Yellow Emperor of China wrote, "I have heard that in ancient times the people lived to be over a hundred years, and yet they remained active and did not become decrepit [broken down] in their activities."[1] His impression was probably inaccurate, however, and humans actually lived only about thirty years. With improved agricultural systems and the rise of cities, average human life expectancy rose to about thirty-eight years. The classical Greeks (roughly 500 B.C.–336 B.C.) and Romans (about 50 B.C.–A.D. 410) lived about thirty-five years, the drop due to increased travel and the spread of diseases such as tuberculosis and smallpox.

Life expectancy rose to about forty-eight years in the early Middle Ages with the growth of cities but dropped again after the Black Death wiped out a quarter of Europe's population. Beginning in the 1800s life expectancy began a steady climb, with better public health, vaccines, better food preservation, and better access to health care. Today both men and women can expect to live well into their eighties. Centenarians, people living to see one hundred years, are now more common than ever before.

Challenges for the Future

Just as the Industrial Revolution changed society in the nineteenth century, a medical revolution changed it in the nineteenth and twentieth centuries. As the twenty-first century dawns, medicine is faced with a new set of challenges unforeseen just one hundred years ago. One challenge is meeting the health needs of an exploding world population. Rapid advances in medicine and health in the twentieth century led to increased birth rates, more babies surviving infancy, fewer people dying from infectious diseases, and people living much longer than they used to. In the fifty years from 1950 to 2000, the world's population more than doubled, ballooning from about 2.5 billion to over 6.2 billion.

Despite the tremendous capacity of modern medicine to heal, there is still a huge inequality in its delivery. Even in the United States, high-quality health care is largely a privilege of those who can afford its skyrocketing costs, while those who cannot must settle for lower quality or no health care at all. As medical care becomes more expensive to the patient and more costly for the provider, there is concern that cutting costs will lead to cutting corners and that quality and availability of health care will suffer for it.

With advancing medical technology such as genetic engineering, cloning, and stem cell research come issues of ethics and morality that must be addressed. Are the benefits of such technologies worth their cost? Is medicine overstepping its bounds and "interfering" in natural processes? These and other questions are being debated both inside and outside the medical community. Meanwhile, health-care providers face challenges such as the health-care needs of an increasingly elderly population, the emergence of new infectious diseases such as AIDS and the Ebola virus, and the reemergence of old diseases such as tuberculosis and cholera. These and other issues will characterize the face of medicine in the future.

Chapter One

The Beginning: Primitive and Ancient Medicine

I n the beginning, according to the lore of many ancient cultures, life on earth was blissful and peaceful, without trouble or care. The eighth-century B.C. Greek poet Hesiod wrote that life was "without evils, hard toil, and grievous disease." Then, for some reason, everything changed, and "thousands of miseries roam among men, the land is full of evils, . . . diseases come upon men, some by day and some by night, and they bring evils to the mortals."[2] The ancient Greeks explained the arrival of disease and death with the legend of Pandora's box, in which Pandora, the first woman on earth, is given a jar containing all the evils of the world. Although commanded by Zeus not to open it, her curiosity overcomes her and she opens the jar, unleashing all the evils upon humankind. In the Judeo-Christian tradition, a similar story is told of Adam and Eve, who live in paradise until they disobey God by eating fruit from the forbidden tree. God casts Adam and Eve out of paradise, and all humankind thereafter must experience hard labor, pain, disease, and death.

Health and Illness in Prehistoric Times

The stories about Adam and Eve and Pandora, with their descriptions of an earlier time without disease and death, may have a certain element of truth to them. The earliest humans were hunters and gatherers, living in nomadic, or wandering, family groups of thirty to forty individuals. As long as populations remained low, they were probably fairly well nourished.

Most infectious, or spreadable, diseases caused by organisms such as bacteria or viruses were likely almost unknown to primitive humans, because these organisms need large, dense populations of susceptible animals, such as humans, in order to reproduce themselves. Because they were nomadic, primitive humans did not stay long enough in one place to pollute water sources with human waste, and they did not keep domestic cattle or other animals that might carry diseases that could be transmitted to humans through their meat or milk.

The major threat to the health of primitive people came from injuries such as broken bones and deep wounds. Wounds caused by accidents or animal attacks could cause death from blood loss, or they could become infected from organisms living in the soil. Predatory animals such as wolves could spread diseases such as rabies through their bite. Parasites such as worms also caused illness in primitive humans. Other threats to health included climate change leading to famine, conflicts with other wandering groups, and childbirth. A group member who became ill or injured presented a major problem for a group that needed to be almost continually on the move in order to survive. Such unfortunate individuals were most likely abandoned rather than cared for by the other group members.

Primitive Treatments

It is unknown how these earliest human ancestors treated their illnesses and injuries. Some writers have suggested that early humans may have imitated self-care methods they observed in animals, such as licking wounds, relieving stomach upset by eating plants to force vomiting, or lying in cool water to relieve pain. Early humans may also have learned to slow bleeding by applying

pressure to the wound. There is archaeological evidence to suggest that prehistoric humans knew how to set fractured bones. Bone calluses, or scars, show that some bones healed well (though not always straight), whereas others show signs of infection after being broken.

There is also evidence from the Neolithic period (10,000 B.C. to 7000 B.C.) that early man performed a procedure called trepanation. This involves making a hole in the skull, either by boring or drilling the hole or by removing a piece of the skull. Examination of some

Ancient Greeks attributed the origins of disease and death to the myth of Pandora's box. When Pandora opened a locked box against the wishes of the gods, all manner of misfortunes were released.

This skull from approximately 2200 to 2000 B.C. shows four healed trepannings. Trepanning is the most ancient form of surgery.

trepanned skulls shows evidence of healing around the hole, indicating that the procedure could be done successfully, even then. It is not known why this was done. It may have been a religious ritual, because it was done on both living and dead subjects, and because the removed skull pieces were sometimes worn as an amulet or charm. It may have been done to release evil demons or to relieve severe headaches.

Health, Illness, and the Rise of Agriculture

Over tens of thousands of years, populations of early humans steadily rose, and the availability of food sources became more of an issue. Gradually, primitive tribes migrated out of the African continent in which they originated into Asia and southern Europe. By around 10,000 B.C. they had crossed from Asia into North America via a land bridge, created by lower ocean levels during the last ice age, which ended about thirteen thousand years ago.

Over the next four thousand years, as the climate warmed and the polar ice caps melted, sea levels rose again, making further widespread migration impossible. No longer could humans survive by eating whatever was available and then moving on to the next place. When game animals and edible plants eventually became scarce, they were forced to stay in one area and learn to grow their own food and build more secure shelter. Humans learned to create and use tools for these purposes. As humans learned to cultivate crops, they also learned to domesticate animals such as cattle, pigs, sheep, goats, poultry, and dogs. Within a few thousand years, hunter-gatherers had been almost entirely replaced by farmers.

The so-called agricultural revolution made it possible for humans to feed themselves more reliably than they ever had before, and human populations rose rapidly, but there was a downside. According to Roy Porter, a professor of social history:

> Many of the worst human diseases were created by proximity to animals. Cattle provided the pathogen pool with tuberculosis and viral poxes like smallpox. Pigs and ducks gave humans their influenza, while horses brought rhinoviruses and hence the common cold. Measles, which still kills a million children a year, is the result of rinderpest (canine distemper) jumping between dogs or cattle and humans. Moreover, cats, dogs, ducks, hens, mice, rats, and reptiles carry bacteria like Salmonella, leading to often fatal human infections; water polluted with animal feces also spreads polio, cholera, typhoid, viral hepatitis, whooping cough, and diphtheria.[3]

Besides promoting disease-causing bacteria and viruses, human settlement also led to infections with parasites such as roundworms, hookworms, and the blood fluke *Schistosoma*, which causes the deadly disease schistosomiasis. Stored food attracted insects, fungi, and rats. According to Porter, agriculture also led to a reliance on grains as a large portion of the human diet. This kind of diet, high in calories but low in protein and vitamins, led to vitamin-deficiency illnesses such as pellagra (vitamin B deficiency), marasmus (protein deficiency), and scurvy (vitamin C deficiency).

The Emergence of Epidemics

Despite the rapid increase in the occurrence of disease, birth rates still outpaced death rates, and human numbers continued to rise. By 3000 B.C. cities with populations numbering in the tens of thousands had arisen in areas such as Egypt, the Indus Valley (present-day Pakistan and parts of Afghanistan and Iran), and Mesopotamia, the land along the Tigris and Euphrates Rivers in present-day Iran. As civilizations grew, however, so did contact between communities. Traders and travelers brought illnesses from one area to another, and the era of epidemics began.

An epidemic is an unusually widespread outbreak of a particular disease. When a specific disease-causing organism, such as the virus that causes smallpox, arrived in a new community, an epidemic could result, often killing off a large percentage of the population. Those fortunate enough to survive would develop immunity, a natural resistance to the illness. Eventually, there would be so few vulnerable individuals left that the epidemic would burn itself out there, and the organism would appear in a more vulnerable community, carried there by traveling humans or their animals. Epidemics became more common with the rise of the Roman Empire, beginning in the first century A.D. With their military conquests in Greece, Persia, northern Africa, and Europe, illnesses such as smallpox, malaria, dysentery, and measles killed thousands.

As cities continued to grow in size, human populations expanded quickly enough that there were always sufficient numbers of vulnerable individuals, and diseases such as measles, smallpox, and

A city in chaos from an illness. The formation of cities led to epidemics, widespread outbreaks of specific diseases that killed off large numbers of people. Many survivors developed immunity to the specific disease.

chicken pox became endemic—the organisms stayed in the area rather than moving on to a new community. With these organisms always present, humans became more resistant to them, and deaths from them declined. Other diseases, especially those carried by animals, were much more lethal to humans, and deadly epidemics of bubonic plague, malaria, and yellow fever continued to devastate human populations.

With human populations becoming more stable and less nomadic, a shift occurred in the attitude toward the sick and injured. Rather than being abandoned, as they had been during the time of the hunter-gatherers, sick or injured people were cared for within their families. There arose the need to have community members who had special abilities in caring for the sick and injured, and medical care became an occupation.

The First Healers

With the development of agriculture and the growth of cities, human society became more complex. Languages, both spoken and written, became more sophisticated. Religious rituals that honored early gods and spirits became more structured and intricate. With no real way to explain how illnesses happened, early societies tended to attribute them to evil spirits or angry gods. As the need arose for certain individuals to take on specific functions within the community, the role of religious healer became an important one.

Ancient religious healers were called shamans. They were considered to have divine powers, including healing the sick, foreseeing the future, ensuring fertility in women, and guaranteeing a successful hunt. A shaman would help the sick or injured person by casting magical spells or by calling upon the spirits or gods to heal the person. Special objects called amulets or talismans were used for good luck or to ward off evil spirits. Healers also began to make use of medicines such as alcohol, opium, and tobacco to help ease pain, relieve fevers, increase energy, and restore health.

Mesopotamian Medicine

By the time of the Bronze Age, beginning around 4000 B.C., Mesopotamia had become the site of some of the world's earliest great civilizations. The repeated flooding of the two rivers made the land around them very fertile, and agriculture flourished there, along with the large human populations necessary to cultivate the land and harvest the crops. In Mesopotamian cultures, as in most other ancient cultures, illness was most often blamed on the spirit world: A person might be possessed by an evil demon that could strike the person with illness or even death. An angry god might use illness to punish a person for some kind of wrongdoing. An angry relative might be accused of using sorcery or witchcraft to get revenge on a person by making him or her sick. Even the dead could cause trouble for the living if they had died an unnatural death or if memorial offerings were considered inadequate by the dead person's spirit.

Paleopathology

Paleopathology is the study of ancient illness and injury through examination of archaeological evidence such as bones, teeth, and other remains. The term was coined in the nineteenth century by Sir Marc Armand Ruffer (1859–1917) and comes from the Greek roots *paleo*, meaning "ancient," *pathos*, meaning "suffering" or "disease," and *ology*, meaning "branch of knowledge." Scientists such as archaeologists, geneticists, and anthropologists may participate in paleopathology studies. Advanced technology such as CAT (computerized axial tomography) scans, electron microscopes, and fiber-optic light instruments may be used to examine remains.

Most archaeological evidence exists in the form of bony skeletal remains and teeth, but some remains may include hair, skin, organ tissue, and even blood. Soft tissues such as organs and muscles usually do not survive over time, except in some cases of mummified remains, but no bodies older than Egyptian mummies from 4000 B.C. have been found. Close examination of ancient remains has uncovered evidence of many human diseases and conditions that existed in antiquity, including tuberculosis, leprosy, syphilis, parasite infections, arthritis, bone tumors, malnutrition diseases, tooth infections and cavities, urinary infections, and pneumonia. The dangers of pregnancy and childbirth are evident in remains of women found with unborn babies still tightly wedged in the pelvic bones, or found with infants buried beside them. Ancient skeletons reveal evidence of injuries such as broken bones and skull fractures, as well as evidence of surgical procedures such as trepanation of the skull.

One of the earliest cultures to thrive in Mesopotamia was that of the Sumerians. By 3100 B.C. the Sumerians had built large cities, erected magnificent temples to their gods, and developed an early form of writing called cuneiform. Much of what is known about Sumerian culture, including its medical practice, has been learned from deciphering cuneiform tablets. One important source is a code of laws and legal decisions written by the Babylonian king Hammurabi (1792 B.C.–1750 B.C.). Carved on a huge stone pillar over 8 feet (2.4m) tall, the Code of Hammurabi is the earliest known written set of laws. Ten of its 282 laws regulate medical practice. They determine such things as what healers should be paid for their services and what the punishment would be if a patient died after surgery. Both payment and punishment were much greater if the patient were wealthy than if the patient were a slave.

Assyria was another ancient Mesopotamian kingdom. In the 1920s approximately 660 medical tablets from the library of the Assyrian king Ashurbanipal (685 B.C.–627 B.C.) were translated. In addition, 420 tablets from the library of an unnamed Assyrian healer have been translated. Most of these tablets are in the form of prescriptions for particular patients, but many others are treatises (informational writings) and describe a wide variety of diseases and ailments, as well as what kinds of plant, animal, and mineral substances should be used to treat them.

There were two main kinds of Mesopotamian healers. The *ashipu*, the Mesopotamian version of the shaman, were exorcists or sorcerers. They were responsible for diagnosing an illness, determining which spiritual cause was responsible for it, and using whatever magic spells or charms were necessary to get rid of the demon, appease the angry god, or undo the evil spell. They were also responsible for interpreting omens and preparing temples for religious ceremonies. The *ashipu* often worked together with the other type of healer, the *asu*.

The *asu* were priests who relied more on practical, hands-on treatments than on spiritual practices, and they were sometimes referred to as a physician as well as a priest. They were experts at herbal remedies, treatment of injuries,

The stele of the Code of Hammurabi (1792–1750 B.C.) contains ten laws for regulating the practice of medicine.

and some surgical procedures. Plants were used extensively, especially for intestinal, skin, and respiratory ailments. Many plants were known to help prevent or cure infections, and spices were sometimes used to mask the odor of an infected wound. They might be crushed or dried, then mixed with some fluid such as wine, beer, or water. For example, one Mesopotamian medical text includes this prescription: "If a man's tongue is swollen so that it fills his mouth, you dry tamarisk leaves, leaves of the adaru plant, leaves of fox grape (and) dog's tongue plant; you chop them up finely and sift; you knead them with juice of the kasu plant; you rub the top of his tongue with butter; you put (the medication) on his tongue, and he will get well."[4]

The *asu* treated injuries by washing them, applying a plaster made of medicines, and then bandaging them. The *asu* could also be a surgeon. Clay tablets describe an *asu* cutting into a patient's chest to drain pus. Another mentions his use of a knife to scrape the patient's skull. The *asu* could also set broken bones and drain abscesses (pus-filled sores) and may have used bloodletting (opening a vein to let blood out) as a treatment. Even so, knowledge of human anatomy was probably limited because dissections (cutting and examining bodies) were not done.

The Mesopotamians could not have known about germs and their relationship to disease, but they did understand that illnesses could be spread from one person to another. A letter written between 2000 B.C. and 1500 B.C. by a person name Mari illustrates this knowledge:

> I have heard that the woman Nanna is ill with simmum disease [translated as either "skin disease" or "serious disease"], but she has nevertheless been in contact a great deal with the palace servant women and she has infected a great many of the women around her. Give strict orders that no one drink from a cup she drinks from, that no one sit on a chair she sits on, and that no one sleep in a bed she sleeps in so that she does not infect any more of the many women around her. That simmum disease is easily caught![5]

The Egyptians

The ancient civilization of the Egyptians, located in northeastern Africa along the Nile River, lasted from around 3200 B.C. until around 525 B.C. This civilization was remarkably advanced compared to other areas of the world at that time. The regular flooding of the Nile deposited a layer of rich, fertile silt on the land each year, supporting a flourishing agricultural society. The ancient Egyptians were accomplished metalworkers, had their own systems of writing and mathematics, had a well-developed body of art and literature, carried on trade with neighboring societies, maintained a strong military force, and carried out massive building projects dedicated to their gods. A complicated

Imhotep

Imhotep ("one who comes in peace") is one of the best-known figures of ancient Egypt. Estimates of his birth vary from around 2655 B.C. to around 2630 B.C. Born a commoner, his intellect and skills allowed him to rise through the ranks of Egyptian society to become an important member of the courts of as many as four pharaohs. He is the world's first named architect and is credited with building Egypt's first pyramid, the step pyramid at Saqqara, located just south of Cairo and the oldest of the seven wonders of the ancient world. He was also a high priest to the sun god Ra, a scribe, a poet, an astrologer, and chief minister to the pharaoh Djoser (also called Zoser, 2630 B.C.–2611 B.C.). As one of the world's first-known physicians, he is best known for his medical texts. He is thought by some historians to be the author of the famous Edwin Smith Papyrus. Imhotep is known to have diagnosed over two hundred diseases, including tuberculosis, appendicitis, gallstones, and arthritis. He practiced surgery and treated wounds. He understood the function of many of the body's organs and was an expert in the use of medicinal plants. One hundred years after his death, around 2600 B.C., he was made a demigod, and in 525 B.C. he was elevated to the status of god of medicine and healing. He was honored by the ancient Romans, worshipped by the ancient Greeks, and even worshipped by some early Christians.

In addition to his medical expertise, Imhotep was also a renowned architect who designed and built the step pyramid at Saqqara.

Written in 1570 B.C., the Ebers Papyrus is the oldest preserved medical document and contains over seven hundred formulas for preparing traditional remedies.

hierarchy of priests, scribes, and other officials maintained the social order within a strict code of religious beliefs, but ultimate rule was the privilege of the pharaoh, who was considered a god as well as a man.

Ancient Egyptians were very concerned with health, cleanliness, and the prevention of illness. Dietary restrictions, regular bathing, and purification rituals were everyday practices. Like other ancient cultures, illness was often attributed to evil spirits or angry gods, and a major task of the Egyptian priest-physician was to identify the evil spirit or demon responsible for the patient's ailment and drive it out. A patient might be treated with herbal remedies, bandages for a wound, or surgery, as well as magical spells and charms. A wide variety of plant substances such as aloe, garlic, mustard, licorice, mint, and many others were prescribed for ailments like insomnia, headache, fevers, burns, constipation, and bleeding. Animal products such as honey, milk, and even animal feces and urine treated night blindness or respiratory and skin problems. Gold wires were used to secure loose teeth.

Medical practitioners, both men and women, were an important part of Egyptian society. Egyptian physicians were highly valued and sought after by people throughout the ancient world. In his classic work *The Odyssey*, the Greek poet Homer writes, "In Egypt, the men are more skilled in Medicine than any of human kind."[6] A complicated hierarchy of physicians existed, with the chief physician at the top, followed by such titles as master of physicians, inspector of physicians, director of physicians, plain physicians, and a number of assistants and support staff. Egyptian doctors were highly specialized. In the fifth century B.C., the Greek historian Herodotus wrote of Egyptian medicine, "The art of healing is with them divided up, so that each physician treats one ailment and no more. Egypt is full of physicians, some treating diseases of the eyes, others the

head, others the teeth, others the stomach and others unspecified diseases."[7]

Egyptian physicians kept detailed records of their observations and treatments. Much of what is known about ancient Egyptian medicine comes from written scrolls made from papyrus, a paper-like material made from reeds. One of the most important of these is the Edwin Smith Papyrus, written around 1600 B.C. Both its beginning and end are missing, so it is not known who wrote it, though some scholars suggest that a much older version may have been written by the Egyptian physician Imhotep (around 2655 B.C. to around 2600 B.C.). The papyrus is unusual for writings of the time in that it approaches medicine from a more scientific angle rather than a religious or magical one. It deals almost exclusively with surgical procedures and the treatment of traumatic wounds. It is divided into forty-eight specific cases describing injuries and procedures for most parts of the body, with titles such as "Instructions concerning a gaping wound in his head, penetrating to the bone and splitting his skull"[8] and "A gaping wound in the throat penetrating to the gullet [food tube]."[9]

Another important source is the 110-page Ebers Papyrus, written around 1500 B.C. Like the Edwin Smith Papyrus, it is thought to be a copy of a much older work. The Ebers Papyrus differs from the Edwin Smith in that its first three chapters describe approximately seven hundred magical incantations designed to chase out evil spirits. It includes information on anatomy, including twenty chapters called "The Book of the Stomach," and a description of the heart and blood vessels (although ancient Egyptians believed that the vessels carried all the fluids of the body, including tears and urine). It provides extensive information on ailments of almost every part of the body, from hair to toes.

Another important source of information about ancient Egyptian medicine comes from studying Egyptian mummies. The practice of embalming the dead, or mummification, dries the body and preserves it so well that even after thousands of years, intact tissue and hair remain, as well as bones and teeth. It was not uncommon for an embalmer to examine the body during mummification to try to determine what caused the death and to record his findings. Egyptian mummies show evidence of diseases such as tuberculosis of the spine, arteriosclerosis (hardening of the arteries), polio, various birth defects such as clubfoot and dwarfism, pneumonia, urinary tract infections, dental cavities, and intestinal parasites.

Ancient Eastern Medicine—India and China

Medicine also has a long history both in the Middle East and the Far East. From the early Iron Age in India (approximately 1800 B.C.) comes a text known as the Atharva Veda, the first-known medical writing from India. A sacred text of the Hindu religion, the Atharva Veda is made up mostly of prayers and hymns for health and long life, good fortune, appeasement of gods, success in warfare, marriage, funerals, and family life. The first part deals with the healing arts and the use of both black and white magic to rid people of demons. It identifies causes of maladies such as fevers, coughs, skin sores, leprosy, parasitic worms, broken bones, and even mental illness and paralysis, and includes prescriptions for using herbal remedies and magical spells. A charm for perfect health, for example, says in part, "From thy eyes, thy nostrils, ears, and chin—the disease which is seated in thy head—from thy brain and tongue I do tear it out. From thy neck, nape of the neck, ribs, and spine—the disease which is seated in thy forearm—from thy shoulders and arms I do tear it out. From thy heart, thy lungs, viscera, and sides; from thy kidneys, spleen, and liver we do tear out the disease."[10]

During the first thousand years B.C., the oldest known organized system of health and healing appeared in India. Known as Ayurveda, or "knowledge of long life," it is built on the philosophies of Buddhism and Hinduism. Ayurveda is a holistic approach to health, which means it is designed to help people lead a long, healthy life by maintaining balance in the body, mind, and consciousness through proper diet and lifestyle, as well as the use of plant-based remedies. The most important Ayurvedic texts come from two healers called Charaka and Sushruta, both born around 600 B.C. The writings of both men contain information on physical examination, diagnosis, and treatment of illness.

The Yin and Yang of Health

In traditional Chinese philosophy, the concept of the *yin yang* means that in nature, opposites exist that may seem contradictory to each other but are actually necessary to the existence of each other. Each aspect of the yin yang is part of a whole. For example, there can be no dark without light, no high without low, no hot without cold, no front without back, and so on. Yin yang is commonly symbolized by the *taijitu*, the familiar circle with both black and white halves. Yin is thought to represent cold, dark, weak, slow, wet, and passive characteristics and is associated with water, earth, the moon, and night. Yang represents hot, light, strong, fast, dry, and aggressive characteristics and is associated with fire, the sky, the sun, and day.

In traditional Chinese medicine, all the parts of the body are considered to be interrelated. Yin dominates certain parts, such as the soft abdominal organs and the body fluids. Yang dominates the head, the spine, the skin, and the muscles. Health results when the yin and yang are balanced. This balance is constantly fluctuating, however, and any imbalance in yin and yang that is not corrected results in illness. For example, a person who is frequently angry and aggressive is dominated by yang. When he or she returns to a calmer state, yang returns to balance with yin. Practitioners of traditional Chinese medicine try to determine where the imbalance is in the yin and the yang and correct it with acupuncture, herbal remedies, diet, and exercise.

The philosophical concept of yin yang refers to the existence of opposites and extremes in nature. They may appear contradictory, but each supports the existence of the other by providing balance.

Charaka's text, called the Charaka Samhita, stresses the importance of the holistic approach of balance in order to prevent illness. For example, he says that "a physician who fails to enter the body of a patient with the lamp of knowledge and understanding could never treat diseases. He should study all the factors, including environment, that influence a patient's disease and then prescribe treatment. It is more important to prevent the occurrence of disease than to seek a cure."[11] Sushruta's writings describe 125 surgical instruments and 300 surgical procedures, such as amputations, repairing facial deformities and bone fractures, and treating cataracts (clouding of the lens of the eye). Ayurveda is still practiced today, and modern medical science has shown that many of its methods are effective for reducing blood pressure, lowering anxiety, slowing aging, and speeding recovery from illness.

The beginnings of Chinese medicine are hidden in the myths and legends of thousands of years. The most important ancient medical text from China is called the *Inner Canon of the Yellow Emperor*. It is attributed to the emperor Yu Hsing, who lived around 2600 B.C. According to the *Inner Canon*, illness is caused by an imbalance or disruption in the flow of energy, called the chi through the body. This disruption was often diagnosed by close examination of the person's pulse, which was thought to be the basis for all medical diagnosis. Harmony in the chi is restored through religious ritual and herbal remedies. Another treatment, well known still today, is acupuncture, which uses very fine needles, placed in strategic parts of the body, to restore the flow of chi.

Much of traditional Indian and Chinese medical practices are considered today to be valuable and useful, although most American and European physicians do not consider them substitutes for standard Western medicine. Coming later but overlapping ancient Eastern medicine was the medicine of the Greeks and Romans. Physician-philosophers such as Hippocrates, Aristotle, and Galen brought entirely new concepts of health and illness to the world—concepts that would guide Western medical thought for centuries.

Chapter Two

Greek and Roman Medicine

Sometime in the seventh or eighth century B.C., the people living in what is today Greece adopted the alphabet that had been developed by the Phoenicians around 1500 B.C. and adapted it into the Greek alphabet. (The word *alphabet* comes from the first two Greek letters, alpha and beta.) This period, known as the archaic period of Greek history, lasted until around 500 B.C. It marks the beginning of Greek civilization, especially in its art and its political ideas about democracy.

The classical period of Greek history began around 500 B.C., when the Greeks came into conflict with the Persian Empire to the east, and lasted until around 336 B.C., after the death of the conqueror Alexander the Great. At this time Greece was not a unified nation as it is today but was a collection of independent city-states, such as Athens, Sparta, and Thebes, each with its own government. During this time Greek civilization reached the height of its achievements in philosophy, politics, architecture, literature, and the arts. The classical period saw the full development of democracy, the building of the Parthenon and the Acropolis, the rise of Greek theater, and the development of the schools of philosophy established by Plato and Socrates. The classical Greeks were also accomplished scientists, making major strides in astronomy, physics, mathematics, and medicine. It is with the Greek civilization that medicine began to evolve into an organized science, with observation of the patient, philosophies about nature, and rational thought playing an important part in medical ideas.

The Beginnings of Greek Medicine

Although the ancient Greeks respected the medicine of the ancient Mesopotamians and Egyptians, it is not known how much influence they actually had

A cast of an ancient Greek gem depicts a physician examining a patient while the god of medicine, Asclepius, leans on his snake-coiled staff—the symbol of medicine.

on Greek medical thought. Unlike the Egyptians, the early Greeks had no established medical hierarchy, and anyone could practice as a healer. There were no written medical codes or lists of instructions like the Mesopotamian Code of Hammurabi. In fact, very few Greek texts about medicine exist from before the fifth century B.C. Ancient Greek literature tells heroic stories about battles with other civilizations such as the Persians and describes how battle wounds were treated. In the epic poem the *Iliad*, written by the poet Homer sometime in the early eighth century B.C., a physician is summoned to tend to the wounded King Menelaus of Sparta. Homer writes, "When they had now arrived where fair-haired Menelaus

had been wounded . . . instantly thereupon he extracted the arrow from the well-fitted belt. But while it was being extracted, the sharp barbs were broken. . . . When he perceived the wound, where the bitter shaft had fallen, having sucked out the blood, he skillfully sprinkled on it soothing remedies."[12]

Greek medicine was not based on religion as much as in other ancient cultures, but there was a spiritual aspect to it. Certain gods were given healing qualities. Apollo, a part of both Greek and Roman mythology, was called the god of healing. The warrior and physician Asclepius, the son of Apollo and a human mother, was said to have the power to raise the dead. After his death Asclepius was raised to the status of a god. Temples to him appeared in cities throughout Greece, and institutions for medical education were called *aesclepia*. Other religious healers included priests, exorcists, and shamans. Some diseases, especially seizure disorders such as epilepsy, were considered punishment from the gods.

Hippocrates and the Humoral Theory

Despite the reliance on gods and mythical heroes, most Greek medical thought was not based on religion but instead on observation and careful study. The first Greek medical school was established around 700 B.C. At this school the medical writer and philosopher Alcmaeon wrote one of the first known works on anatomy (the study of the structure of the body) sometime between 500 B.C. and 450 B.C. He was one of the first to suggest that illness was caused by problems with environment, nutrition, and lifestyle choices. His study of the nose, ear, and eye led him to conclude, correctly, that the brain is linked to the sense organs and is the source of consciousness and intelligence.

In the fifth century B.C., Greek medicine began to develop as a true scientific discipline, with written observations, case histories (descriptions of specific patients and their illnesses), and structured medical education. Medical schools were built on the island of Kos and in the city of Cnidus. From these schools came a philosophy about health and illness that completely rejected the influence of religion and supernatural forces. This school of thought, called Hippocratic medicine,

began with the work of the great Greek physician and philosopher Hippocrates (around 460 B.C. to 377 B.C.), often called the father of modern medicine. Most of what is known about Hippocratic medicine comes from a collection of about sixty texts, written by Hippocrates and others, which were collected together into what is called the Hippocratic Corpus (body of work).

The Hippocratic philosophy of health and illness was based on reason, rational thought, and the laws of nature, rather than on supernatural or religious forces. Very little was known about human anatomy and physiology (the study of the internal workings of living things) because dissection of human bodies was forbidden. Emphasis was placed on building a trusting relationship with the patient, providing good patient care with gentle treatment, making a careful diagnosis of the problem, and determining the prognosis, or the probable outcome of the disease. Hippocrates wrote, "It appears to me a most excellent thing for the physician to cultivate Prognosis; for by foreseeing and foretelling, in the presence of the sick, the present, the past, and the future, . . . he will be the more readily believed to be acquainted with the circumstances of the sick; so that men will have confidence to intrust themselves to such a physician."[13]

The core ideas of Hippocratic philosophy reflected what the Greeks observed and believed about nature—that it is balanced and stable but also changeable. Hippocrates believed that the body had the power to heal itself, that allowing nature to take its course, with the doctor mostly waiting and watching, was the best course of action, and that rest, a clean and peaceful environment, and maybe a soothing balm were the best ways to treat illness. He taught that an illness would eventually reach a crisis, at which time either the illness would prevail and the patient would die or the body would heal itself and the patient would recover.

Hippocrates also believed that balance between certain body fluids (the Greek word was *chymoi*, translated as humors) was essential for good health. Disease was seen as a result of an imbalance of the humors. There were four main humors, or influential fluids, in the body—blood, yellow bile, black bile, and phlegm. Each humor was associated with an element—air, fire, earth, and water—and with one or two of the four qualities— hot, dry, cold, and wet (first introduced by the Greek philosopher-scientist Aristotle). A person's health—and even appearance, intelligence, and personality—could be explained by the particular way in which his or her four humors were combined. In each type of person, one of the humors would dominate. For example, people with a lot of blood were sanguine (loving, optimistic, and peaceful). Those with too much phlegm were phlegmatic (stern, unemotional). Those with too much yellow bile were

The great Greek physician and philosopher Hippocrates is considered the father of medicine.

choleric (angry, irritable), and those with too much black bile were melancholic (sad, pessimistic).

Diagnosis of disease was based first on listening closely to what patients had to say about their illness, followed by careful observation of the patient's facial expression, skin color and texture, temperature, and body fluids such as blood, urine, and mucus. Humoral treatments such as bloodletting (opening a vein to

Ancient Historians— Herodotus and Thucydides

Much of what is known about the ancient world comes from the works of two major writers of the time, Herodotus and Thucydides. Herodotus (around 480 B.C. to around 420 B.C.) was born in Helicarnassus, in present-day Turkey. He is sometimes called the father of history because he is the first-known writer to have carefully gathered his information and test its accuracy before recording it in a logical and systematic fashion. His major work, *The Histories*, written around 440 B.C., is a sweeping account of the Greco-Persian wars in the fifth century B.C. *The Histories*, divided into nine volumes, provides extensive information about the culture, warfare practices, politics, philosophies, and personalities of several ancient Mediterranean civilizations, including Egypt, Greece, Assyria, and Persia. Book 2 discusses the medicine of the Egyptians, and the work includes varied descriptions of battle wounds and their treatment. It is said that Herodotus was so proud of *The Histories* that he read the entire work aloud to the crowd at the Olympic Games held at Olympia. Some accounts of this event mention that in the crowd was a young Athenian named Thucydides, who was so fascinated by the reading that he burst into tears.

Thucydides (around 460 B.C. to 395 B.C.) was a wealthy Athenian who is sometimes called the father of scientific history because of his meticulous attention to historical evidence and analysis based on realistic observation. In his major work, *History of the Peloponnesian War*, Thucydides wrote extensively about the conflict between Athens and Sparta, also in the fifth century B.C. While in exile from Athens after a military defeat, he spent twenty years among the Spartans and their allies, so he was able to make firsthand observations of the war from both sides. He survived the Plague of Athens and wrote vivid descriptions of its symptoms and effects on Athenian society. Thucydides and Herodotus became close friends and had high respect for each other. Some accounts say that both of them are buried in Thucydides's tomb in Athens.

let blood out), laxatives (to cause bowel movements), emetics (to cause vomiting), and enemas (to cleanse the intestine) were designed to restore the balance of the humors. Changes in diet, sleep habits, and lifestyle were prescribed. Drugs were rarely used, and any medicines given were based on the person's unique makeup of humors. Although Hippocratic physicians knew about surgery, it was a last resort and was left to others who had more experience with it.

The Legacy of Hippocrates

Although most of Hippocratic medical thought has been discredited today, Hippocratic physicians made several important contributions to modern medicine. Their emphasis on healthy diet, exercise, and lifestyle are still basic to maintaining health. Their methods of examination and observation are still cornerstones of modern medical practice. Hippocratic physicians were the first to describe clubbing of the fingers, a sign of long-term heart and lung disease. They described diagnosis and treatments for problems in the intestinal tract and procedures such as cautery (burning) and ligation (tying) that are still used today. Hippocrates wrote extensively about empyema, a severe infection of the lining of the chest. The Hippocratic Corpus includes descriptions of treatments for head injuries and other wounds, the importance of releasing pus from infections, the care of fractured bones, and the treatment of bladder stones.

With the help of the conquests of the Greek conqueror Alexander the Great (356 B.C.–323 B.C.), the influence of Greece spread around the Mediterranean Sea, from the former Persian Empire to Egypt and into southern Italy and Sicily, which had cultural similarities to Greece. By 300 B.C., Greek had become the dominant language in the area, and knowledge in all areas of human experience grew, including in medicine. Greek physicians in Egypt and Italy performed human dissection and learned the difference between arteries, which carry oxygen-rich blood away from the heart, and veins, which carry oxygen-poor blood back to the heart. They described and named several organs, including the prostate gland and the duodenum, the first part of the small intestine. They wrote on ophthalmology (study of the eye), childbirth practices, and on the anatomy and purpose of the brain, spinal cord, and nerves. They understood the value of the pulse as a diagnostic method. Notably, however, Greek medical practice did not at first become accepted practice in the new center of the world, the city of Rome.

Medicine in the Roman Era

The civilization of ancient Rome overlapped the Greek civilization but began later. The city of Rome itself began as a village on the Tiber River in central Italy sometime in the eighth century B.C. Rome was ruled by kings until around 509 B.C., when the kingdom was replaced by a republican form of government in which leaders were elected by the people. During the Republic, Rome began its conquest of neighboring peoples. In the mid-first century B.C., Rome was controlled by a series of dictators, including Julius Caesar, until 31 B.C., when the dictator Octavian took the name Caesar Augustus and became the first emperor of Rome. During the time of the Roman Empire, Rome expanded its rule into Asia, Africa, and as far north as modern-day England, reaching its peak in power and territory in the second century A.D.

In the early years of the Roman era, the Romans adopted little of Greek

Aristotle

Aristotle was an ancient Greek philosopher and scientist. He was born in 384 B.C., the son of a wealthy physician. He was educated in Athens and eventually became a teacher to the Greek conqueror Alexander the Great. In 335 B.C. he opened his own school, called the Lyceum. Aristotle was interested in a great many different subjects. He wrote extensively about politics and government, history, geography, economics, psychology, religion, and literature. He also had a highly scientific mind and contributed new knowledge in natural sciences such as anatomy (he dissected animals but not humans), astronomy, embryology (the study of the development of animals before birth), physics, botany (the study of plants), and zoology. He developed a complex system of classification of animals, which he divided into animals with blood and animals without blood. He believed that heat was the most important thing for maintaining life and that the heart was the most important organ because it was the source of heat. The lungs and brain, he believed, were for cooling the body.

Aristotle died in 322 B.C. His main contribution to medicine was his beginning development of the scientific method, based on observation of the natural world,

logical thought, and reason instead of superstition. He revolutionized the field of biology by studying plants and animals in their natural habitats rather than in artificial environments. Although many of his ideas were proved incorrect after his death, Aristotle's work in science and philosophy still had a lasting effect on later Christian and Muslim (followers of Islam) thinkers, and he is still considered one of the most influential thinkers and philosophers of the ancient world.

In the fourth century B.C. the influential Greek philospher Aristotle wrote on many topics, including history, economics, and medicine. He developed an early version of the scientific method based on observations of the natural world.

medicine. Romans believed that they were stronger and healthier than the Greeks and therefore had little need for doctors. The Roman statesman and writer Cato (234 B.C.–149 B.C.) cautioned that doctors could only bring death and that Greek physicians "have sworn to kill all barbarians with their drugs."[14] Even after Rome gained control of Greece in the first century B.C. and Greek physicians arrived there, Romans mostly remained in contempt of them and considered them frauds and cheats.

Anyone could practice medical treatment; there were no universities or schools of medicine. Teachers, wise women, midwives, herbalists, and even household slaves served as healers. There were very few physicians, and most of them were immigrants from other areas, such as Asia Minor. While the wealthier citizens might enlist the aid of a physician if necessary, most medical issues were handled in the home, by the head of the household or by a private servant. Romans believed that the individual was responsible for maintaining his or her own health. Philosopher and politician Marcus Tullius Cicero (106 B.C.–43 B.C.) wrote, "It is our duty, my young friends, to resist old age; to compensate for its defects by a watchful care; to fight

The Romans built water-carrying channels called aqueducts to bring water from remote regions to Rome. Public latrines, baths, and sewer systems helped prevent disease.

against it as we would fight against disease; to adopt a regimen of health; to practice moderate exercise; and to take just enough food and drink to restore our strength and not to overburden it."[15]

The Romans and Public Health

The ancient Romans believed that preventing illness in the first place was better than having to treat it. To this end, the ancient Romans were the first civilization to introduce an organized system of public health measures, and it is one of their most important contributions to modern ideas about health and wellness. Although they had no knowledge of germs and other organisms as the cause of disease, they understood that certain conditions were more likely to cause illness, so they took measures to prevent those conditions. Roman scholar and writer Marcus Terentius Varro (116 B.C.–27 B.C.) offered advice about choosing where to build one's home:

> When building a house or farm especial care should be taken to place it at the foot of a wooded hill where it is exposed to health-giving winds. Care should be taken where there are swamps in the neighborhood, because certain tiny creatures which cannot be seen by the eyes breed there. These float through the air and enter the body by the mouth and nose and cause serious disease.[16]

Clean water sources were very important to the Romans. They built water-carrying channels called aqueducts above street level to carry clean freshwater from lakes and rivers into the cities. Public latrines and sophisticated underground sewer systems carried waste and dirty water away from populated areas. Low-lying marshy areas were drained to control insects. Another Roman writer, Lucius Junius Moderatus Columella, explained why: "There should be no marshes near buildings, for marshes give off poisonous vapours during the hot period of the summer. At this time, they give birth to animals with mischief-making stings which fly at us in thick swarms."[17] Personal hygiene was very important to the Romans, and public baths were provided for regular bathing. Food was plentiful and fresh, and like the Greeks, the Romans valued a balanced, varied diet. Even today the Mediterranean-style diet, with its emphasis on lean meats, fish, fresh vegetables, and healthful oils, is considered one of the most beneficial of all diets.

Gods, Greeks, and War

In contrast to the Hippocratic physicians of Greece, the Romans relied more heavily on supernatural and magical remedies for illness. Epidemics of disease were blamed on angry gods, and sacrificial rituals were performed to try to appease them. Herbal cures, spells, and charms were common methods for healing. Superstition, astrology, and dream interpretation were also relied upon by some practitioners determining causes

In a Pompeian fresco, a doctor is depicted treating a soldier. Physicians gleaned much valuable information about human anatomy and surgical procedures from treating battle wounds.

and cures for illness. Temples were built to Apollo, the god of the sun, medicine, and healing, and to his son, Asclepius, both of whom were revered in Rome as well as Greece.

Much of this changed, however, throughout the late first century B.C. and early first century A.D. This was a time of conquest and increasing military strength, and Emperor Augustus understood the importance of a well-trained medical staff to the success of his army. He created a school for army doctors and recruited them by offering titles, land, and money. Public health measures were applied to the military as well as to the civilian population. Although they had no understanding of germs, they kept their instruments clean between patients. They cleansed wounds with acetum, similar to vinegar, which they had learned prevented infections. Clean, dry, well-ventilated hospitals were created for wounded soldiers. Sewers and drainage systems kept human and animal waste away from the soldiers.

A great deal about human anatomy and surgery was learned from the treatment of battle wounds. Army physicians carried sophisticated surgical instruments, including scalpels, forceps, drills, hooks, saws, and probes. They knew how to use plants with sedative (calming) and painkilling properties. Army doctors knew that bleeding could lead to death, and they were skilled at applying tourniquets (tight bands) and clamps and at tying off bleeding vessels. Information learned from both successful and unsuccessful treatments was recorded and shared with other doctors.

Physicians, including Greeks, gradually gained respect and acceptance in Roman society. Physicians such as Scribonius Largus (A.D. 1–50), who learned medicine on the island of Sicily and wrote a handbook of drug concoctions in Latin, and Celsus (around A.D. 25 to 50), who wrote an extensive encyclopedia that included an eight-volume work on medical topics, brought Greek medical thinking to Rome and its territories. The most important and influential physician of the Roman era, however, was the Greek philosopher-physician Claudius Galen (A.D. 129 to around 200), whose work influenced medical thought for well over a thousand years.

Galen

Part of the reason for Galen's lasting influence was the enormous volume of his writings, much of which still survives. According to medical historian Roy Porter, "More of his opus [written work] survives than of any other ancient writer: some 350 authentic titles ranging from the soul to bloodletting polemics [opinion writing]—about as much as all other Greek medical writings together. He had a vast education and a matching ego."[18]

Galen was born in Pergamon (in present-day Bergama, Turkey) in A.D. 129, the son of an aristocratic architect. He received an extensive and varied education in philosophy, politics, and literature. At age sixteen he was sent to the local *aesclepium* (medical school and temple to Asclepius), where he stayed for four years, learning his craft from treating the wealthy Romans who came there for healing. After his father's death, he traveled widely through Greece and visited the famous library and medical school at Alexandria, Egypt, studying closely the teachings of Hippocratic physicians on diet, physical fitness, and cleanliness. At

Some of second-century physician Claudius Galen's many writings have survived. His wide-ranging works include discussions of the soul, blood and circulation, and the dressing of wounds.

age twenty-eight he returned to Pergamon and became the physician to the gladiators there, learning about human anatomy from treating their battle wounds.

In A.D. 162 he went to Rome to practice medicine, but despite his excellent reputation, he had so many disagreements with the doctors already there that he left Rome. He was called back, however, when the devastating Antonine Plague (thought to be smallpox) struck Rome.

He became the personal physician to Emperor Marcus Aurelius and then to his son Commodus. In A.D. 189 the deadly disease returned, killing as many as two thousand Romans each day. Galen wrote extensively about the symptoms and his treatment of the illness, which is sometimes called the Plague of Galen. After Commodus, Galen served several later emperors. Several accounts of Galen's death exist, but he is thought to have died sometime between A.D. 200 and 216.

Galen's Legacy

Late in his life Galen wrote, "I have done as much for medicine as Trajan did for the Roman Empire when he built bridges and roads through Italy. It is I, and I alone, who have revealed the true path of medicine. It must be admitted that Hippocrates already staked out this path . . . he prepared the way, but I have made it passable."[19] His contributions to medicine are certainly extensive. Through his dissections of animals, mostly pigs and apes, he described the trachea (windpipe) and demonstrated that the larynx is the source of the voice. He wrote a great deal about blood and circulation, including sixteen books about the pulse alone, and observed the difference between venous (dark red) blood and arterial (bright red) blood. He incorrectly

Ancient Plagues

Both the ancient Greeks and the Romans suffered through devastating epidemics of illness that claimed thousands of lives. The first was the Plague of Athens, an outbreak of what is now thought to be typhoid fever, which struck Athens in 430 B.C., during the second year of the Peloponnesian War between Athens and Sparta. The historian Thucydides, who himself survived the illness, wrote at the time that the plague started in Ethiopia in eastern Africa. From there it spread through Egypt and into Greece. He gives a very detailed account of the symptoms, which included headaches, rashes, fever, stomach cramps with vomiting, unquenchable thirst, and coughing up blood. Most victims died on the seventh or eighth day, but those who survived did not get it again. Athenian physicians were unable to help the victims and often became victims themselves. About one-third of the population of Athens died of the illness, including the Athenian military leader Pericles.

The Antonine Plague struck Rome in A.D. 165, during the reign of Emperor Marcus Aurelius Antoninus, who died from it and for whom it is named. It is also called the Plague of Galen, who wrote about it. The disease is believed to have been smallpox, brought to Rome by troops returning from military campaigns in Asia Minor (present-day Turkey). According to Galen, the disease caused fever, diarrhea, sore throat, and a rash that appeared on the ninth day of illness. As the Roman army moved into Europe, the disease went with them, devastating not only the army itself but the European populations they exposed to it. The illness recurred several times and is estimated to have killed approximately 5 million people by the time it ended around A.D. 189. Some historians believe that it contributed directly to the eventual fall of the Roman Empire.

believed, however, that the two were separate systems, that arteries began in the heart and carried air, and that veins arose from the liver. He also wrote about the nervous and respiratory systems and performed surgeries on the brain and eye.

Galen and his writings are credited with carrying Hippocratic medical thought to much of the rest of the world. He developed more fully the Hippocratic notion of the four humors and their influence on health and temperament. After the fall of the western part of the Roman Empire in 476, his work was preserved in the mainly Greek-speaking Eastern Empire, also known as the Byzantine Empire, and eventually influenced Islamic medicine in the ninth century. From there, it spread into Europe, where it remained the dominant force in medical thought until the sixteenth century. Some of his teachings, such as the practice of bloodletting, lasted even into the nineteenth century.

The Greek and the Roman physician-philosophers laid a strong foundation for medicine as a science, with observation of the patient within his or her natural surroundings of prime importance to diagnosis and treatment. As Roy Porter explains, they "created the ideal of the union of science, philosophy, and practical medicine in the learned physician, who would be the personal attendant of the patient rather than a medicine man interceding [pleading] with the gods."[20]

With the decline of these civilizations, however, and the beginning of the time known as the Middle Ages, that kind of inquiring thought almost disappeared. "For the next thousand years or more," says Porter, "medical knowledge would change little. This was partly the consequence of the break-up of the Mediterranean civilizations, but also because of the solidity of these foundations. Galen's enduring reputation was the epitome of these beliefs: he unified theory and practice, discourse and the doctor, but his death brought that tradition to a halt."[21]

Chapter Three

Medicine in the Middle Ages

By the third century A.D., the Roman Empire had become so large that it became almost impossible for one ruler to govern the entire area effectively. In 285 the Roman emperor Diocletian divided the empire into two parts of roughly equal size. The Western Empire included Italy, southern and western Europe, and England. Rome remained the capital in the west and was governed by a separate emperor named Maximian. Diocletian ruled the Eastern Empire, which included Greece, the eastern Mediterranean, and Asia Minor (Turkey). Nicomedia, a city in Asia Minor, was the eastern capital.

Under Diocletian's successor, Constantine, several civil wars took place between east and west. Constantine was ultimately victorious and became the sole ruler of the empire. In 313 he proclaimed the new religion of Christianity to be the preferred religion of the empire. In 324 he moved his capital to the Turkish city of Byzantium, which he renamed Constantinople, in his own honor. Today the city is called Istanbul and is still the capital of Turkey.

After Constantine's defeat of Rome, the Western Empire became the victim of frequent invasions by warlike tribes of people from central and northern Europe and by Asian tribes led by the Mongolian warrior Attila the Hun. In 410 Rome was sacked by a tribe called the Goths, which effectively ended the Western Empire for good. Europe became a collection of small kingdoms ruled by the descendants of the invading tribes. Its cities weakened, and poor peasants farmed the land owned by powerful landowners in their castles. Learning, literacy, and scientific inquiry all but ceased, and Europe descended into an idle period of almost one thousand years that today is known as the Dark Ages.

Health and Illness in the Dark Ages

With the final fall of the Western Empire, civilization in Europe began a slow decline.

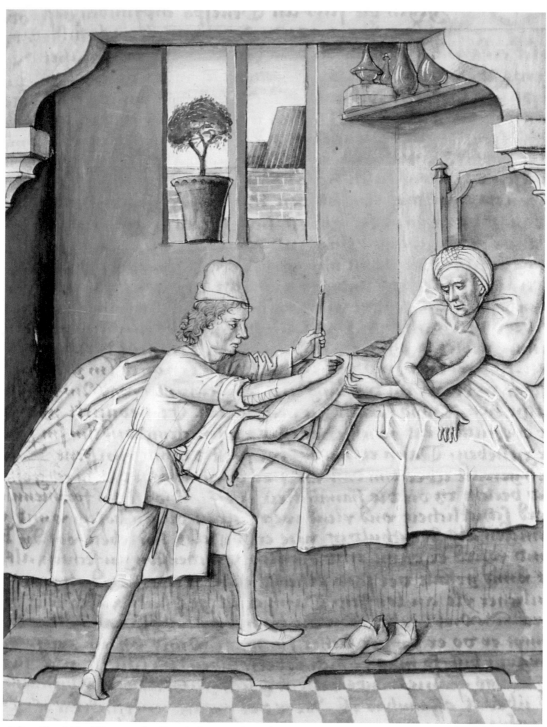

After the fall of Rome, the Dark Ages ushered in an era in which the practice of medicine was largely reliant on the use of such remedies as charms, potions, and exorcisms.

The loss of contact with the East led to an eventual abandonment of most of the learning and knowledge of the Greeks and Romans. Roman public health practices were also discarded. Clean water was scarce, and personal hygiene was almost nonexistent. Illness was a constant problem, and people returned to the ancient pagan beliefs about demons and other supernatural forces as causes of illness. Charms, potions, magical spells, incantations, and exorcism of demons were used to treat the sick. Schools dwindled, and educated physicians almost completely disappeared.

One concept from the Greeks that did remain in practice was the Hippocratic idea of the balance of the four humors, or bodily fluids—black bile, yellow bile, phlegm, and blood. Diagnosis of disease and imbalance of humors was based on the patient's general appearance, examination of his or her blood, feces, and urine, and sometimes checking the pulse. Balance of the humors was maintained by proper diet, exercise, herbal remedies, and bloodletting. Bloodletting remained popular for centuries despite the dangers of infection, worsening weakness, and uncontrollable bleeding leading to death. Despite the lack of anesthesia, surgical procedures included setting bones and amputation of wounded limbs.

Medicine and Religion

By the early fifth century, Christianity had spread to the farthest reaches of the former Western Empire. With the increasing influence of the Christian Church throughout Europe, all aspects of everyday life became controlled almost exclusively by religious authorities, including attitudes about illness and healing. "By contrast with the naturalistic bent of Hippocratic and Galenic medicine," says medical historian Roy Porter, "healing became more spiced with religion, for the rising church taught that there was a supernatural plan and purpose to everything . . . and Christian doctrines, rituals, and sacraments covered every stage through which believers passed from womb to tomb, and beyond."[22]

Whereas the Greeks had taught that body and soul were intertwined, the church taught that they were separate, with the soul taking priority over the body, and medicine and physicians taking a backseat to religion and priests. Illness and pain came to be seen as divine punishment for the wicked or as a test for the faithful. Disease was therefore to be accepted as part of God's plan, and healing was only to be brought about by constant prayer to the saints and by the mercy of God. The old pagan healing practices and traditional folk medicine practices were considered incompatible with Christian faith and were made illegal by the church or replaced with acceptable Christian versions. Dissection of the human body for educational purposes was also condemned, and anyone found guilty of dissection or other mishandling of the dead could be punished by being burned at the stake. The only allowable exception was cesarean section of a

Medieval Women in Medicine

During the Middle Ages, women often served as midwives. They also worked as nurses and as practitioners whose duties were similar to those of physicians.

During the early Middle Ages, women practiced healing arts almost as much as men did. Women served in several roles—practitioners, similar to physicians, midwives, nurses, or local folk healers. Female physicians were uncommon, and in most places there was a distinction between male physicians and female "licensed healers." This was especially true after physicians began to be trained in university medical schools, to which women were not admitted. Most women were expected to remain in the home and serve the health needs of the family. The wives of wealthy landowners were sometimes expected to see to the health needs of the peasants serving on the landowner's estate.

Midwives—practitioners who provided care for women before, during, and after childbirth, were always women. In complicated cases, however, they might ask a physician for help. Midwives learned their craft from older midwives and occasionally from male relatives who were physicians. Midwives sometimes provided charms or magic spells to assist the woman in labor, and for this they were sometimes punished by the church.

Nurses in the Middle Ages were usually women who worked in the hospitals and orphanages. Many, but not all, were nuns in the monasteries. Nonreligious nurses became more common during the time of the Black Death, when the need was greatest and there was a shortage of nuns. Nurses had many more duties than just to feed, clothe, bathe, and minister to the sick. They also cleaned the wards, did laundry, cooked the food, and cared for the dead by bathing the body and preparing it for burial.

dead pregnant woman in order to save the soul of the baby.

Although the Christian Church taught that illness was to be accepted as part of a divine purpose, it also taught that the body belonged to God and therefore had to be taken care of. The church provided healing services and comfort for the sick, administered by the monks and nuns of the monasteries and convents and under the supervision of the local bishop. While some fragments of Hippocrates, Galen, and others were read in the monasteries, care of the sick was mostly limited to basic support, with herbal remedies sometimes used for comfort. Monks were not allowed to leave their monasteries to go to a medical school, and surgery, including bloodletting, was strictly forbidden. Special buildings attached to a monastery or church were built for the sick and the poor. One of the first sick houses was founded in 390 by a wealthy Roman woman named Fabiola. Her teacher, Saint Jerome, wrote of her:

> She assembled all the sick from the streets and highways, and personally attended the unhappy and impoverished victims of hunger and disease. I have often seen her washing wounds which others—even men—could hardly bear to look at. . . . How often she carried home, on her own shoulders, the dirty and poor who were plagued by epilepsy? How she washed the pus from sores which others could not even behold.[23]

Byzantine Medicine

In contrast to the western part of the former Roman Empire, the Eastern Empire (called the Byzantine Empire, after the city of Byzantium) flourished. With larger, more populated cities, a strong military, and an economic structure healthy enough to pay off potential invaders, the Byzantines were spared much of the outside invasion suffered by the west. In the sixth century the Byzantine emperor Justinian managed to reclaim much of the western territory lost to the invading tribes. Under Justinian, Byzantine culture became a dynamic blend of Roman, Greek, European, and later, Arabic traditions. Greek was the predominant language, and Byzantine art, philosophy, literature, and architecture were carried to all parts of the empire.

Greek and Roman writers in the Byzantine Empire preserved and passed on much of the medical writings of Hippocrates and Galen, as well as produced their own work. Physicians recorded what they observed and learned, and they compiled their knowledge into large and elegantly illustrated textbooks. The physician Oribasius (325–397) was one of the most productive writers of the Byzantine Empire. He collected and simplified much of the work of Galen and other earlier writers (including correcting them where he felt they had been wrong) and shared his work with others. His earliest work consisted of four books that address hygiene, diet, the proper use of medications, and a description of health problems in almost all parts of the body.

Byzantine hospitals were large, often containing several wings in which different diseases were treated. Their services included surgical procedures and care for women and the elderly.

Another important Byzantine was Paul of Aegina (circa 625–690). His major work, *Seven Books of Medicine*, is said to contain all of what was known about medicine at the time. The books deal with pregnancy, mental illness, surgery, the elderly, skin diseases, drugs and poisons, and many other subjects. In his *Twelve Books of Medicine*, Alexander of Tralles (circa 525–605) shows that there was still reliance on spells and superstition in the empire. For treating colic in infants, he advises, "Remove the nipple-like projection from the cecum of a young pig [the appendix], mix myrrh with it, wrap it in the skin of a wolf or dog, and instruct the patient to wear it as an amulet during the waning of the moon. Striking effects may be looked for from this remedy."[24]

Under Justinian and later rulers, Byzantine hospitals came to resemble modern public hospitals in several ways. They were large and provided a multitude of services, including care for women and the elderly and surgery. There were separate wings for individual illnesses such as leprosy or mental illness. Like the earlier sick houses run by monks or nuns, hospitals were usually built at or near a church and maintained by the local bishop, and prayer was used in treatment along with drugs and surgery. Physicians were organized into a hierarchy, with chief physicians (men and women), nurses (mostly men), and orderlies. Most physicians were educated at the university in Constantinople, built in 425, and there was an established code of professional practice and behavior for doctors.

Despite their advanced learning and enlightened practices, however, Byzantine physicians were at a loss to cope with the most significant health challenge ever to strike humankind up to that time—the devastating epidemic that came to be known as the Plague of Justinian.

The Plague of Justinian

Plague is a very dangerous and often fatal disease that is caused by a microscopic organism called *Yersinia pestis*, often abbreviated as *Y. pestis*. *Y. pestis* lives in the gut of fleas that live on the body of the black rat and can be transmitted to humans by the bite of the flea. At the time of the Byzantine emperor Justinian in the mid-sixth century, the black rat was everywhere, feeding on the grain, spices, and other products brought on ships to Constantinople for trade.

In 542 the plague appeared in Constantinople, having already caused widespread death in parts of North Africa and the eastern Mediterranean area. It started on the docks, where the rats were most abundant, and quickly spread throughout the city. It killed its victims so quickly that a person who was healthy in the morning could be dead by nightfall. A writer of the time, John of Ephesus, wrote, "Nobody would go out of doors without a tag upon which his name was written and which hung on his neck or arm,"[25] so that the person could be identified if he or she died suddenly.

Byzantine physicians were at a loss to handle a crisis of such magnitude.

Mental Illness in the Middle Ages

Mental illness was very poorly understood in the Middle Ages because it was not understood to be an illness at all. There were no physical symptoms to be observed, and there was no effective treatment. Learned medical men followed Galen's teachings by dividing symptoms into four categories: frenzy (wild or violently agitated behavior), mania (mental and/or physical hyperactivity), melancholy (extreme sadness or depression), and fatuity (stupidity or foolishness). Each type was thought to be caused by an imbalance in the four humors. Many people believed the changing phases of the moon caused insanity; the word *lunatic* comes from *luna*, the Latin word for "moon." Women were thought to be more susceptible than men to mental illness; the word *hysterical* comes from the Greek *hysterus*, meaning "uterus."

The church tended to see mental illness as possession by the devil or other demons. After the terror of the Black Death, blamed by many on Satan, mentally ill people who were thought to be possessed by the devil risked being accused of witchcraft. For almost three hundred years after the plague, as many as fifty thousand people, mostly women, were tortured and executed as witches.

Treatment of the mentally ill varied from place to place. Some communities expelled or banished those who were considered insane. Most were cared for in the home by their families. Others were cared for in monastic hospitals or special "madhouses." The Islamic community provided special hospitals for the mentally ill as early as the eighth century. Common remedies for mental illness included drugs and bloodletting. Some believed the illness could be "shocked" out, perhaps by whipping or by plunging the person into ice water. Fasting, prayer, and exorcism, a religious ritual for ridding the body of demons, were methods used by those who thought the illness was due to demonic possession.

They had no way of knowing what was causing the illness. Their only recourse was bloodletting, herbal remedies, and prayer. None of it worked, and people died by the thousands. The hospitals were overwhelmed with patients, and bodies piled up in the streets, with not enough people left to bury them. Bodies were thrown into the sea, piled in mass graves, or thrown into the guard towers that surrounded the city.

The plague stayed in Constantinople for about four months. Eventually, there were not enough rats or people left for the bacteria to infect. It spread on to Rome and much of the rest of the empire and invaded the neighboring Persian Empire (modern-day Iraq, Iran, Pakistan, and Afghanistan). Waves of it appeared over and over again throughout Europe, the Mediterranean, and the Middle East over the next two hundred years, eventually killing an estimated 25 million people.

From around the twelfth century until the end of the Byzantine Empire in 1453, there was little new medical knowledge coming out of the empire, mostly because of the decreased population after the plague, wars with Arab and Turkish invaders, and two major civil wars within the empire itself. In 1453 the invading Ottoman Turks captured Constantinople, and the Byzantine Empire effectively came to an end. The Byzantines' contributions to medicine, however, remained significant, especially in terms of preserving the works of Galen and Hippocrates and passing them on to Renaissance Europe.

The sharp decrease in population also had lasting effects in Europe, where agriculture was an important part of the economy. With fewer people to work the land, new labor-saving devices such as the plow were improved to make the work more efficient. The shortage of workers also meant that farmers could demand more in wages from the land owners. As a result, farmers became more prosperous, and the population in Europe recovered faster than in other parts of the empire. Europe began a slow reawakening that was to have a great impact on society there. At the same time, in the mid-seventh century, a new religion called Islam appeared in the Arabian Peninsula. It quickly became a powerful political and military force in the area because of the weakened Byzantine and Persian Empires. Islamic culture grew and flourished, and with it, the approach to health and illness.

Islamic Medicine

Islam was founded by Muhammad (570–632), a wealthy merchant from Mecca, the capital city of modern-day Saudi Arabia. Around 610 he received a vision in which the holy book, the Koran, was revealed to him. By the time of his death, Islam had spread over most of the Arab world, and during the next century Islamic armies had conquered much of the Byzantine and Persian lands, including North Africa and Spain. They were not concerned with replacing Christianity or Judaism, however, and until the Christian Crusades of the eleventh through thirteenth centuries, the three religions lived together well.

Before Islam, medicine in the Arab world was similar to medicine in other places. Illness was blamed on evil spirits and genies. Magic, spells, and charms kept evil spirits away. Herbal potions, local substances such as dates and honey, and even camel's urine were common remedies. Bloodletting was employed to balance the humors. Surgery was very simple, and little was known about internal anatomy. Public health measures were scarce, and illness was common; Justinian's Plague

Avicenna

One of the greatest Muslim practitioners was the Persian physician and philosopher Abu Ali al-Husayn ibn Abd Allah ibn Sina (980–1037), called Ibn Sina, or Avicenna in the West. Avicenna's scholarly talents showed early in life; it is said that he could recite the Koran by the age of ten and was a practicing physician by eighteen. He was also a chemist, mathematician, astronomer, teacher, psychologist, and poet. He wrote well over two hundred works, forty of them on medical topics.

His best-known work is his *Canon of Medicine*, a five-volume encyclopedia that includes the entire body of medical knowledge up to that time, including a summary of Hippocrates, Galen, and other Greek, Indian, and Arab writers. The *Canon* includes information on the four humors, anatomy, physiology, and descriptions of many illnesses, with their symptoms, diagnosis, treatment, and prognosis. In the *Canon*, Avicenna writes about the benefits of personal hygiene, exercise, and weight control. He advises doctors on how to treat ulcers, poisoning, fractures, and other injuries. Two of the five volumes are devoted to the collection and use of many drugs, including the importance of testing them to make sure they are safe, and evaluating their effectiveness—revolutionary concepts for the time. Because Avicenna understood that some diseases could be spread between people through social contact, he promoted quarantine for certain illnesses. He also theorized about the existence of microorganisms as the cause of disease. The *Canon* became one of the most important medical texts in the world at the time and was used in European universities for centuries.

In this seventeenth-century illustration, Arabian physician Avicenna has his assistants prepare remedies for smallpox. He wrote an extensive treatise on medicine, the Canon of Medicine.

hit the Arab world as hard as it had the Byzantine and Persian Empires, and large cities such as Cairo and Alexandria in Egypt lost almost half their population. Most educated healers were Christian doctors, but few people could afford their services.

As Islam gained strength through the seventh and eighth centuries, traditional medicine was gradually replaced by more religion-centered views. Although the Koran has little to say about medicine, it was consulted for advice on healing, and prayers were offered up to Allah, the Muslim name for God. In the eighth and ninth centuries, Muslim and Christian scholars began to translate into Arabic hundreds of Greek medical and philosophical texts of Galen, Hippocrates, and others.

Over the next three hundred years, Muslim scholars produced many medical works of their own. Arabic scholars such as Razi (865–925, known as Rhazes in the West), Ibn Sina (980–1037, known as Avicenna), and Ibn Rushd (1126–1198, called Averroës) wrote manuals, essays, and larger encyclopedic works. They wrote about their philosophy of health and illness, anatomy, physiology, pharmacology, surgery and cautery (the use of heated instruments to open skin and stop bleeding), dentistry, pregnancy and childbirth, mental illness, the circulation of blood, and the diagnosis and treatments of problems in all parts of the body. They recognized that several different diseases could cause symptoms such as a rash or a fever. They gained particular fame for their

skill at eye surgery and pioneered the sight-restoring procedure called cataract extraction, the removal of a clouded lens of the eye.

Islamic hospitals were patterned after the sick houses of the monasteries, and all patients were cared for, regardless of age or religious faith. Several hospitals, mostly in the larger cities, were large and complex, with many services offered, including surgery, mental health care, pharmacies (the first in the world), and libraries. There were also separate hospitals just for the mentally ill, where humane and compassionate care was offered. Most new doctors learned their craft in schools attached to the hospitals, under a master physician. Students spent much of their time memorizing texts, following older physicians on their rounds, and performing simple procedures such as bloodletting. Dissection of the human body was strictly prohibited; what they knew of anatomy came from earlier writings, care of open wounds, and close observation of the patient.

In all that they did, Muslim physicians wrote detailed, well-organized records of their observations of their patients and allowed reason and logic to guide their decisions. Scientific inquiry, reason, clinical observation, and careful record keeping became hallmarks of Islamic medical practice. After around 1300, with the loss of lands to the Christians and the Turks, the Islamic golden age began to decline. Islamic achievements in medicine, however, continued to earn great respect in universities throughout Europe. The practices of Muslim physicians survived, especially in the Islamic world, until the advent of modern Western medicine in the nineteenth century.

Rebirth in the West

Beginning around 1100 medical thought began a slow revival in the West. This is the time known as the High Middle Ages, when the population grew steadily and trade with other parts of the world expanded. Universities appeared and became centers of learning, and hospitals grew in size and number, offering more services to the growing population.

As the population of Europe grew, the need arose for a better-educated clergy. In 1079 Pope Gregory VII issued a decree that ordered the establishment of schools for this purpose.

The earliest universities began as these cathedral schools. Over time more and more students came to these schools to study theology (religious studies), logic, philosophy, law, debate, and medicine. The University of Bologna in Italy was founded in 1088, followed by the University of Paris in 1110 and Oxford (in England) in 1167. Other, less religious universities also appeared. At these universities, the ancient classical writings of Aristotle, Galen, and Hippocrates were revived and translated into Latin. With the reconquest of Islamic Spain by the Christians, Europe gained access to some of the Arabic world's best libraries, and scholars began the translation of Arabic texts, including medical texts.

Despite the renewed interest in the Greek classics and in Arabic medical knowledge, medicine remained firmly under the control of the Catholic Church. Monasteries continued to be centers of healing. Religious orders of knights such as the Knights Templar built their own hospitals. Shrines were built for prayer to many healing saints like Saint Luke, Saint Christopher, and Saint Michael.

Over the next four hundred years, hospitals grew in number, size, and the variety of services offered. The larger hospitals had their own staff physicians, educated at the increasing number of universities throughout Europe. Private physicians cared for the nobility and the wealthy, while the general population could see a public physician hired by the town government. As hospitals grew and physicians became more numerous, the medical community began to organize itself into guilds, or skilled groups, with rules for training new doctors, regulating herbs and drugs, and insuring professional behavior.

Another consequence of the increasing population, especially in the larger cities, was overcrowding and problems with public sanitation. By the 1300s most cities had responded to this issue by passing laws requiring sewers for waste, as well as clean-water delivery systems. Streets were paved over, and livestock was kept confined to separate buildings. Despite these measures, illness was still very common. In 1347 the most catastrophic health crisis since the Plague of Justinian struck Europe—the Black Death.

The Black Death

The Black Death was an epidemic of bubonic plague that swept through Europe in the mid-1300s. It began in China and moved rapidly westward, following trade routes, until it arrived in Italy in 1347. From there it spread across Europe in a matter of months. Death came very quickly to those infected with the illness, and the symptoms were terrifying. It began with fever and chills, severe headache, sore throat, and muscle aches. Later on there might be vomiting, diarrhea, seizures, bleeding from the mouth or nose, and difficulty breathing. After a day or two, the patient would develop large, very painful swellings, called buboes, in the neck, armpits, or groin. The buboes could split open and emit a foul-smelling drainage. Destruction of blood

An engraving from 1348 depicts the Black Death in Europe. Early symptoms included fever, chills, and sore throat, followed by vomiting, diarrhea, and seizures, and ultimately by the appearance of buboes that split open to emit foul odors.

vessels caused tissues to die and turn black, which gave the disease its nickname.

Death from plague came from massive internal bleeding or respiratory failure. Whole towns were wiped out. Those who managed to avoid infection were too afraid to tend to the sick, for fear of getting the illness themselves. As in Constantinople eight hundred years earlier, there were not enough graves to handle all the dead, and bodies piled up in the streets.

Medieval people were at a loss to explain the cause of the disease. The church had taught that illness was divine punishment for sin, but this one affected people of all kinds, the good and the bad, young and old, rich and poor. Physicians had no explanations either. The humoral theory was still dominant in medicine, and physicians reasoned that if the body was healthy, one should not get sick. The plague proved them wrong as previously healthy people also became ill. With no answers and no help coming from either medicine or religion, people turned to other conclusions. Some blamed it on an unfortunate alignment of the planets. Others claimed it was caused by foul air, or miasma, from swamps, manure piles, or the breath of the sick. Some claimed that the water and air had been deliberately poisoned by "enemies" such as beggars, the insane, or Jews.

For treatment, physicians could offer little more than herbs, potions, and bloodletting. No known treatments for illness worked on this disease. Prayers, visits to holy shrines, and fasting (going without food) were also useless. People were so terrified that they tried almost anything to avoid getting sick. Family members and friends abandoned the sick. Those who could afford it left the cities and sought escape in the clean air of the countryside. People carried flowers or herbs to ward off the scent of the "evil" air. They closed their windows and doors as tightly as they could. They tried blasting the bad air away with loud horns or cannon fire. They set bonfires to try to burn it away. Nothing worked.

The Black Death had a profound effect on European economic, religious, and medical structures. By the time it finally subsided in the early 1350s, almost a quarter of Europe's population was gone. Villages were deserted, and farms crumbled. Skilled craftsmen were scarce, and prices for the products they made skyrocketed. Landowners had to pay their peasants more money to farm their land or risk losing them to other landowners.

Because of the failure of religion to stop the plague, the church lost much of its power and influence with the people. Many religious figures—priests, monks, nuns, and so forth—had died in the plague, and many of those who survived abandoned their congregations to escape it. Disillusioned with their faith, people began to meet in their homes rather than in the churches, and new traditions developed that were different from traditional church teachings.

The medical community also changed as a result of the Black Death. Learned university physicians lost some of their respect as people turned back to local community healers who practiced their craft with a more hands-on approach, instead of relying on unobservable concepts like humors and miasmas. Doctors tested their ideas to see if they really worked or not. Autopsies and dissection of the human body became more common despite the church's objections, and

With the church powerless to stop the plague, many people blamed women for the pestilence, torturing and burning them as witches. As many as fifty thousand people, mostly women, suffered this fate.

much was learned about the internal organs and how they work.

Before the Black Death came, Europe had been locked into a stagnant social structure of poverty, ignorance, and religious oppression. The Black Death changed the structure of European society in so many fundamental ways that this pattern was finally broken. People began to think more about their present lives on earth than about their afterlives in heaven. Europe entered a period of inquiry, learning, and innovation known today as the Renaissance.

Chapter Four

Medical Awakening: The Renaissance

The word *renaissance* means an awakening, a rebirth, or a revival. In historical terms the period known as the Renaissance was a time of renewed political, economic, religious, artistic, and scientific inquiry and learning. It began in Italy in the late 1300s and spread throughout Europe over the next three hundred years.

The Renaissance was marked by a renewed interest in the classical literature of the Greeks and Romans, but with new interpretations of them based on rational thought and observable evidence. The revived interest in non-Christian literature did not mean that Renaissance thinkers rejected Christianity, but there was a shift away from total spiritual control over people's lives by the church and religious officials toward a more secular (nonreligious) and humanist view of life, which maintains that individuals can have control over their own lives. Early Renaissance writers such as Dante Alighieri

(1265–1321) began to use more local languages, rather than just Latin, so that ordinary people could read and understand their work without relying on Latin-speaking church officials to interpret it. With the invention of the printing press in the mid-1400s, books, especially the Bible, became more easily accessible to more people.

In politics and government, there was renewed interest in the democratic, people-driven form of government created by the Greeks and Romans. In art the shift was reflected in the Renaissance artist's appreciation of the beauty and structure of the human form. Painters and sculptors like Leonardo da Vinci (1452–1519) and Michelangelo (1475–1564) produced a more realistic portrayal of the human body and its surroundings. Paintings lost the flat, cartoonish look of the early Middle Ages and took on a more natural, three-dimensional appearance.

The city of Florence, Italy, in 1490. As cities regained their populations after the plague, society became more urbanized and prosperous, with commerce replacing the old economic system of peasants farming land for fuedal landlords.

As the cities regained their populations after the Black Death, society became more urbanized, with trade and commerce replacing the old economic system of peasants farming the land belonging to landlords. The wealthy merchants, bankers, and tradesmen of Europe got used to having luxuries such as gold, spices, and silk, which came from the Orient. The overland trade routes that brought such imports to Europe became restricted as Islam gained strength and Arabic tribes took control of the territory; thus the need arose to find new sea routes. This led to what is now called the age of discovery—an age of exploration that reached its highest point with the discovery of the North and South American continents—the New World.

Columbus, the New World, and Disease

According to historian Roy Porter, the arrival of Europeans in the New World set in motion a health crisis even worse than the Black Death of the fourteenth century. Porter explains:

> The most momentous event for human health was Columbus's landfall in 1492 on Hispaniola (now the Dominican Republic and Haiti). The Europeans' discovery of America forged contact between two human populations isolated from each other for thousands of years, and the biological consequences were devastating, unleashing the worst health disaster there has ever been, and precipitating [leading to] the

conquest of the New World by the Old World's diseases.[26]

Before the arrival of the Europeans, the native peoples of North and South America lived much as the hunter-gatherers of the last ice age had lived. Like those earlier peoples, individual tribes had little contact with each other, and they knew very little about disease. As Central and South American civilizations such as the Mayan, Incan, and Aztec grew, some diseases that go along with an increasing population, such as tuberculosis, occasionally appeared, but still the people were relatively free of illness. They had no experience with European diseases, and their bodies had no defense against them when they were brought by the Spaniards beginning in 1492.

The first serious illness brought to the New World was possibly influenza, thought to have been carried there by pigs on board Columbus's ships. It struck the native Arawak people of Hispaniola and Santo Domingo in 1493 and killed thousands of them (along with approximately twelve hundred Spaniards). The Catholic bishop Bartolome de las Casas wrote a detailed account of the effect of the illness on the population of the islands. "Hispaniola is depopulated, robbed and destroyed," he wrote in 1516, "because in just four months, one third of the Indians . . . have died."[27] In another account written in 1552, he wrote:

> On Saturday 29 March [1494], the Admiral [Columbus] arrived at La Isabela and found the people of La

Isabela were in sad condition because few of them had escaped being sick or dying. . . . Don Bartholomew Columbus [Columbus's brother] in arriving in Isabela found that almost 300 [Spaniards] had died of different diseases. Witnessing the plight of the Indian every day was even worse. There was so much disease, death, and misery, that innumerable fathers, mothers, and children died. . . . Of the multitudes on this island in the year 1494, by 1506, it was thought that there were but one third of all of them left.[28]

Other Spanish conquerors and their diseases quickly followed. Smallpox arrived in the New World in 1518, followed by measles in 1519. These illnesses all but wiped out the Aztec of Mexico and the Inca of Peru. By 1600 typhus had killed an estimated 2 million people in Mexico. To replace the almost extinct native populations, the Spanish brought African slaves to fill the labor shortage. The slaves brought malaria and yellow fever to the New World. All of these diseases contributed significantly to the eventual conquest of Central and South America by the Spanish.

In North America the Indian population was also devastated by European diseases brought by the French and English. Having seen what disease had done in Mexico, the Caribbean, and South America, it was not unknown for the Europeans deliberately to infect blankets, clothing, and other goods with smallpox in order to weaken the native tribes. The Europeans often justified this behavior as divine providence, acceptable in the eyes of God. For example, the Reverend Increase Mather wrote in 1680, "The Indians began to be quarrelsome . . . but God ended the controversy by sending the smallpox among the Indians."[29]

The spread of disease between Old World and New was not only one way, however. It is thought that when Columbus returned from the Americas, he and his sailors brought back with them the sexually transmitted disease syphilis, called the "great pox" to distinguish it from smallpox. Beginning in 1493 epidemics of syphilis raged throughout Europe for the next twenty years. Its symptoms were horrifying, with rashes, skin ulcers, and abscesses that destroyed bone and disfigured the face. It was often fatal. Treatment for syphilis included heating patients to make them sweat, applying an ointment made from mercury to the sores, and the ever-popular bloodletting. The mercury treatment caused excessive drooling and sweating and included severe side effects such as gum sores, tooth loss, and weakened bones. For many the treatment was almost as bad as the disease.

The discovery of the New World by Columbus soon led to more explorations to other parts of the world. Many of these explorations, like those of Columbus, were designed to find new trade routes and bring new wealth to Europe. Others had the goal of spread-

Columbus's men brought with them to the New World germs against which native peoples had no natural immunity. In 1493 thousands died of European diseases in Hispaniola and Santo Domingo.

ing Christianity to native populations. Still others were done simply to learn more about the world. Vasco da Gama of Portugal found a new route to India by sailing around the southern tip of Africa. Ferdinand Magellan, also of Portugal, was the first to circumnavigate, or sail completely around, the world, which proved that the world was round, not flat as was previously believed. Spanish conquistadores (conquerors) such as Juan Ponce de León, Hernán Cortés, and Francisco Pizarro explored the inland areas of North and South America. The French, English, and Dutch all sent expeditions to the New

A sixteenth-century engraving depicts various methods used by Native Americans in an attempt to ward off European diseases. These remedies were fruitless, and millions of natives died.

World and into the Pacific, discovering previously unknown lands such as Australia and the Hawaiian Islands.

Science, the Renaissance, and Medicine

The explorations during the age of discovery brought to Europe not only more economic wealth, but also a wealth of new knowledge about the geography of the world and the cultures of the people who lived in it. The new knowledge added to the desire to learn—a scientific spirit—that had already begun in the earlier years of the Renaissance. A scientific spirit leads to scientific inquiry, which means approaching learning with a fair and open mind, asking lots of questions, considering all possibilities, and drawing conclusions from close observation, research, and testing.

In medicine scientific inquiry meant that if one were to decide that a particular disease had a particular cause, that cause must be tested to prove that it actually leads to the disease. The concept of the four humors remained strong during the Renaissance, and bloodletting to restore balance was still a common treatment for many illnesses, but many physicians questioned whether the four humors could really explain all maladies, especially new illnesses such as syphilis and the English "sweating sickness" (which killed thousands in the late 1400s and early 1500s and is thought by historians to be a strain of influenza). Waves of plague also continued to ravage Europe well into the 1700s; an especially severe one killed almost eighty thousand Londoners in 1665–66. New ideas about the causes and treatment of illness appeared. For example, in an idea that seems to predict the discovery of germs, the Italian physician Girolamo Fracastoro (1478–1553) explained contagious diseases in terms of invisible "disease seeds" that could infect people from a distance or by contact with articles such as clothing.

The Protestant Reformation and Medicine

In the early part of the Renaissance, medicine still remained largely under the control of the Christian Church. The church still held to the teachings of Galen, and few physicians questioned this. Also, the great majority of universities were founded and controlled by religious orders. As the Renaissance progressed, however, traditional thinking was coming into question within the church itself. One of the most important events affecting the evolution of medicine during the Renaissance was the Protestant Reformation.

Led by a monk named Martin Luther, the Reformation began in 1517 as an attempt to reform the Christian Church. The church had become corrupted by many clergy who used their positions in the church to gain power and wealth. Also, wide differences in opinion about religion had arisen among the clergy because of the new humanistic thinking about the role of religion in people's lives. These problems eventually led to a split in the church into Catholics and reformers. The reformers became known as Protestants (those who protested), and they completely rejected the authority of the Catholic Church. In some countries, such as Germany, Norway, Sweden, and Holland, Protestantism became the official religion, and their rulers closed Catholic institutions, including the hospitals. In England King Henry VIII also rejected the Catholic Church, and from 1536 to 1541, he closed the monasteries, seized church-owned lands and property, and drove out the monks and nuns who had cared for England's sick and poor.

Without Catholic hospitals, there was a severe shortage of people to care for the sick. Health care in these countr' suffered, and health institutions bec' unsanitary, poorly staffed places v

A women's ward in a Catholic hospital in San Matteo, Italy. The Protestant Reformation brought about a decline in the ability of the Catholic Church to operate its hospitals.

care was provided mostly by untrained women who came from the lowest ranks of society. In response to this, new, nonreligious medical schools were built, paid for by wealthy patrons other than the church, such as King Henry VIII, who founded Trinity College in 1546.

Anatomy and Surgery

Like the artists and sculptors of the time, Renaissance physicians were very interested in the structure of the human body. As a result of the increased inter-est, anatomy as a science soon gained a larger place in the university medical schools. Dissection was the best way to learn about the inside structure of the human body, but the church had always frowned upon the procedure. In 1482, however, Pope Sixtus IV decreed that dissection of cadavers was acceptable as long as the person was a criminal and was given a Christian burial afterward. Men of various backgrounds, such as Leonardo da Vinci, an artist and sculptor, and Andreas Vesalius (1514–1564), a university-trained physician, performed dissections of human cadavers (sometimes in public) and drew detailed anatomical diagrams of muscles, nerves, blood vessels, internal organs, and many other body parts.

Leonardo da Vinci, despite having no medical training at all, was not only a gifted artist but also a brilliant anatomist. In addition to studying the anatomical structure of all parts of the body, he also studied their function—how they move and work. He studied the development of the unborn baby in the womb and used hydrodynamics (the study of liquids in motion) to explain how the heart moves blood through the body. One of his acquaintances wrote of him:

> This gentleman has written of anatomy with such wealth of detail, illustrating by his art both limbs and muscles, nerves, veins, and ligaments of the inward parts, and of all that may be demonstrated in the bodies of men and women, in a way that has never been equaled by anyone else. And this we have seen with our own eyes, and he has also told us that he has dissected more than thirty bodies of men and women of different ages.[30]

Andreas Vesalius, on the other hand, had extensive medical training in Italy and went on to teach in several Italian schools. He was the author of one of the most influential books on human anatomy, *De Humani Corporis Fabrica* (*On the Fabric of the Human Body*), in which he used what he learned through dissection to dispute almost everything Galen had written about anatomy. He is considered the founder of modern human anatomy because of his accurate, scientific approach to anatomy and the extensive work he did on almost every part of the human body.

Other books and essays on anatomy were being published all over Europe. Many of them addressed very specific body parts, such as the ears, the kidneys, or the valves in veins. One of the most important was English physician William Harvey's (1578–1657) book *De Motu Cordis* (*On the Motion of the Heart and Blood*). Harvey's work on the circulation of blood was very controversial at the time, because many physicians still believed strongly in Galen's work from fifteen hundred years earlier. Galen had written that the heart's function was to produce heat and that arteries carried air and cooled the blood, got rid of bad "vapors" through pores in the skin, and were part of a separate system from veins. Harvey directly contradicted what Galen had concluded, showing that blood circulates through vessels that are part of one system with the heart and that the heart is a simple pump for the blood. Surgery before the Renaissance was considered a lower class of healing art, and surgeons were not considered to be doctors at all but more like craftspeople, in the same class as barbers. In fact, many so-called barber-surgeons performed simple surgical procedures such as bloodletting, pulling teeth, and cutting the umbilical cord after

Leonardo da Vinci, Renaissance Man

Leonardo da Vinci (named for the town of his birth, Vinci, near Florence) was born in 1452. He showed artistic promise early, and at fifteen his father sent him to study art in Florence. He soon proved to be more talented than his teacher, and at twenty-five he set up his own business. He went to work painting and sculpting for the Duke of Milan. He also showed a talent for science and mechanics and produced writings and drawings on a multitude of subjects, including architecture, geology, geography, botany, machines of all kinds, mathematics, music, medicine, and human anatomy. He drew early versions of parachutes, helicopters and airplanes, military tanks, submarines, and rifles. He was especially fascinated by anatomy and spent hours dissecting cadavers to discover how they worked. He began recording his observations in notebooks, including very detailed drawings and diagrams, and often wrote from right to left in backward "mirror writing." (The reasons for this are unknown, but one theory is that he wanted to keep his ideas secret from church authorities. Another is that, being left-handed, writing left to right caused his hand to smear his ink.) After the Duke of Milan lost power, Leonardo traveled through Italy working for various people, including the

pope and King Francis I of France. Among his most famous works are *The Last Supper* (1498) and the *Mona Lisa* (1506). His sketch of the human body called the *Vitruvian Man* (1487) is one of the most reproduced sketches in art history.

Leonardo da Vinci died in 1519. He never had any formal education. He knew no Latin or Greek. He was a natural genius with an unquenchable curiosity about a great many things. His intellectual and artistic accomplishments have led historians to call him a true Renaissance man.

In addition to his talents as a painter and sculptor, Leonardo da Vinci produced written works and drawings in the fields of science, anatomy, and mechanics.

childbirth. (The traditional barbershop pole of red and white symbolizes blood and bandages.) In the 1700s educated physicians who wanted to perform surgery separated themselves from the uneducated barbers, created their own guilds, and gained more prestige. Expressing his belief that surgeons should be of higher character and skill than barbers, English surgeon John Halle wrote that "a [surgeon] should have three divers properties in his person, that is to say, a heart as the heart of a lion, his eye like the eyes of an hawk, and his hands as the hands of a woman."[31]

Hippocrates said that "he who wishes to be a surgeon should go to war."[32] Just as in the time of the Greeks and Romans, much of what surgeons knew in the Renaissance was learned from treating war wounds on the battlefield, but the transition from the swords and arrows of antiquity to guns and cannons in the 1300s created a whole new set of injuries to deal with. Gunpowder weapons caused much more extensive injuries with greater loss of blood and body parts. New ways of treating these wounds were discovered. For example, renowned French surgeon Ambroise Paré (1510–1590) learned that a dressing made with egg whites, rose oil, and turpentine worked much better to prevent "corruption" (infections) in gunshot wounds than the traditional one made with scalding hot oil. He also developed the use of ligatures to tie off damaged blood vessels.

In the civilian community, surgeons dealt mostly with superficial problems such as broken bones, burns, shallow wounds, tumors, amputations, and skin ulcers. There was a wide variety of surgical instruments designed for specific purposes. Bleeding was controlled with cautery, chemicals called styptics, and pressure. In a time before anesthesia, blood transfusion, and antibiotics, surgery was an agonizing and dangerous experience.

Hospitals and Pharmacies

Hospital care in Renaissance England had suffered a major setback after the Protestant Reformation. Until the 1700s, London, with over two hundred thousand people, had only two general hospitals for the sick, one for orphans, one for the poor, and one for the mentally ill. Most people could not afford to go to these larger hospitals, however. As a result, physicians began providing advice about how people could safeguard their health by eating and drinking in moderation, taking regular exercise, and keeping the mind occupied with creative pursuits.

In the cities of Catholic countries such as Italy, Spain, and France, however, hospitals were still mostly run by religious communities and supported financially by wealthy families. As the population of these countries increased, hospitals there became increasingly specialized, with institutions and homes built specifically for children, the poor, the elderly, the mentally ill, and those with specific disabilities such as blindness or infectious diseases such as plague. In general, they were clean,

Renaissance Nursing

Despite the growth of universities and medical schools during the Renaissance, there was still almost no training for nurses. Most women who worked in health care were midwives or worked in the monastic hospitals. In England, after the dissolution of the monasteries by King Henry VIII, women went into charity work or remained at home and provided care for their own families. Hospital work was not appealing for the higher classes, so most hospital nursing was done by female prisoners, alcoholics, or others of lower social status. Nursing came to be seen as a lower-class occupation.

During the sixteenth and seventeenth centuries, the rapid increase in population in Europe after the Black Death created overcrowded cities, with serious sanitation problems and widespread disease. After the Protestant Reformation and the weakening of the Catholic monasteries, the poor and homeless poured into the cities, making the problems worse. Concern for the poor, especially children, led to the creation of several religious nursing organizations. In France, for example, the Order of the Visitation of St. Mary (1610), and St. Vincent DePaul's Daughters of Charity (1633) provided visiting nurses as well as nursing education for young women, including the use of medicines and simple surgical procedures. Both organizations still exist today.

comfortable places where all patients, including the poor, abandoned women and children, and those with incurable illnesses, could receive quality health care. Most hospitals had their own vineyards as well as vegetable and flower gardens, and patients enjoyed fresh food and wine served daily. According to history professor John Henderson of the University of London, "The traditional image of pre-modern hospitals as hell-holes where people were brought to die has been overturned. Hospitals in this period provided free treatment, a warm environment and specialized care, which they would not have found in the community."[33]

The science of pharmacy also changed during the Renaissance. At this time pharmacy became a separate discipline from other areas of medical practice, and universities began to include pharmacy as a separate subject of study. Pharmacists, called apothecaries, became specialists in the preparation of medicines. Just as in other areas of Renaissance medicine, apothecaries approached their craft scientifically. They carefully weighed and measured the amounts of ingredients used in their preparations. They clearly prescribed the length of time that the medicine was to be used. They closely observed and recorded the effectiveness of their medicines and changed the "recipes" as necessary to make them work better.

The great majority of medicinal treatments still were made from plant sources, and the European voyages of discovery added many new choices for the apothecary. From the New World, cocoa made from coca beans became not only a popular drink among Renaissance Europeans but was also used as a stimulant for constipation and a treatment for "wasting diseases" (cancers). Sarsaparilla and sassafras were used for skin problems, arthritis, and the sores of syphilis. Tobacco was introduced to Europe as a treatment for a multitude of symptoms. Quinine made from the cinchona tree was effective for treating malaria symptoms. The Spanish in the Caribbean learned from the native people that medicine made from the wood of the guaiac tree could be used to treat a mild form of syphilis. Considering the unpleasantness of the mercury treatment, the guaiac treatment caught on quickly, and it came to be called "holy wood."

During the Renaissance, pharmacology became a discipline separate from other areas of medical practice. Known as apothecaries, pharmacists became specialists in the preparation of medicines.

From the East, opium became popular as a painkiller and treatment for dysentery and lung problems. Chinese rhubarb, ginseng, aloe, camphor oil, ginger, and cinnamon from the Orient all had medicinal benefits.

In addition to plants and the substances made from them, the Renaissance apothecary also used chemical substances as medicines. For example, mercury was used to treat venereal diseases such as syphilis. Antimony, a highly toxic substance in large amounts, caused vomiting and diarrhea in order to restore healthful balance in the body. Salt was used to treat skin diseases and digestion problems, and also worked like antimony to restore balance. Sulfur was effective for treating infections (just as sulfur-based antibiotics are today). Theriacs, first made by the ancient Greeks as an antidote to poisons, were combination drugs made with as many as sixty different plant, animal, and chemical ingredients. Collecting and preparing all of its ingredients could take weeks or months. The "recipe" varied, depending on who made it and what it was being used for. Besides treating poisoning, theriacs were used to clear blocked intestines, clear up skin ailments, improve strength, promote sleep, cool fevers, and many others. They were also tried as a treatment for plague during the Black Death of the mid-1300s.

Renaissance Medicine Moves Toward the Modern Age

In the sixteenth century religion had already undergone an upheaval with the Protestant reformation. At the same time, "medical protestants" began to offer new and rather controversial ways of thinking about medicine. One of the earliest and most influential of these was named Paracelsus.

Paracelsus, meaning "greater than Celsus" (referring to the Roman Celsus, who wrote about medicine in the first century A.D.), was the name adopted by Theophrastus Philippus Aureolus Bombastus von Hohenheim (1493–1541). Paracelsus, a Swiss botanist, physician, and astrologer, was a strong believer in astrology and the occult and believed that invisible forces intervened between man and God. Nature was the most important thing to him; he believed that observation, experimentation, and experience with nature was the source of all truth and that nature was unknowable to bookish university-educated professors.

Paracelsus infuriated most physicians of his time with statements such as "When I saw that nothing resulted from [doctors'] practice but killing and laming, I determined to abandon such a miserable art and seek truth elsewhere."[34] He ridiculed textbooks and dismissed dissection as a waste of time because it showed nothing about the workings of the living human body. His contempt for traditional classical thinking came out in his writing: "Let me tell you this, every hair on my neck knows more than you and all your scribes, and my shoe buckles are more learned than your Galen and Avicenna, and my beard has more experience than all your high colleges."[35] He publicly burned a copy of

A believer in astrology and the occult, Paracelsus was an early Protestant physician who thought that invisible forces intervened between man and God. He led the way in the treatment of diseases by chemicals.

The Microscope

The invention of the microscope was a gradual achievement, with contributions by several scientists. By the early Middle Ages, the use of convex (thicker in the middle than at the edges) pieces of glass to make small objects appear larger had existed for centuries. In 1284 convex lenses were made into spectacles that could be worn on the face. In the late 1500s, Dutch father and son spectacle makers Hans and Zacharias Janssen began experimenting with glass lenses. They put two lenses into a tube, one near the eyepiece (the ocular lens) and the other near the object to be studied (the objective lens). Their instruments were approximately 2 feet (60cm) long, cumbersome, and heavy, but they magnified objects much more than earlier single-lens instruments.

Other inventors such as Marcello Malpighi (1628–1694) made their own versions. Malpighi used his microscope to observe tiny blood vessels and named them capillaries, confirming William Harvey's theory about the continuous circulation of blood. He also described in detail the anatomy of the lungs, kidneys, brain, bones, liver, and skin. Dutchman Antoni van Leeuwenhoek (1632–1723) is often referred to as the father of microscopy for his significant improvements to the microscope and for the discoveries he made with it. He made his lenses out of quartz instead of glass and made them almost spherical in shape. He observed blood cells moving through capillaries and was the first to see microscopic organisms, which he called "animalcules," in pond water. English scientist and inventor Robert Hooke (1635–1703) used his microscope to confirm Leeuwenhoek's findings and to observe plant cells. He is given credit for coining the term *cell*. Despite the great advances made in microscopy in the seventeenth century, it was almost two hundred years before it found practical applications in medicine.

Avicenna's *Canon of Medicine* and other traditional Galenic texts.

Paracelsus believed in the idea of the four humors, but felt that it was inferior to his own idea of three "spiritual" substances—mercury, sulfur, and salt—which he called the *tria prima*. He thought of these not as actual chemicals, but as qualities of objects as well as people. Sulfur represented the soul and emotions, salt represented the physical body, and mercury represented the spirit and morality. The physician had to understand the interaction of the *tria prima* in order to cure disease. More than other physicians, Paracelsus included in his treatments chemicals such as iron, arsenic, lead, mercury, and copper. He created the pain-killing laudanum, made from opium, and gave the metal zinc its name.

As controversial as Paracelsus was, his work had great influence on the scientific thinkers who followed him. His rejection of traditional thinking led others to publish their own nontraditional ideas about science and medicine. For example, two years after the death of Paracelsus, Andreas Vesalius published his work on anatomy in *De Humani Corporis Fabrica*, and Nicolaus Copernicus (1473–1543) published his revolutionary work on the solar system. Thanks to Paracelsus, medical chemistry, or alchemy, became widely adopted by physicians all over Europe as another option for treatment.

By the end of the seventeenth century, medical thought was undergoing a major transformation. Enlightened thinkers began to cast off the ancient Hippocratic and Galenic ideas of the past, which had no support from the observations physicians were making through experimentation, dissection, and the aid of the recently invented microscope. The next two centuries, often referred to as the age of reason or the age of enlightenment, brought radical changes to medicine, as scientific inquiry led to many important new discoveries.

Chapter Five

Medical Revolution in the Age of Reason

The movement away from the medieval interpretations of Galen and Hippocrates that began during the Renaissance continued at a rapid pace through the next two centuries. This period is known as the Enlightenment, or the age of reason. During this time scholars, scientists, and philosophers continued to question traditional customs and ways of thinking. Reason, logic, science, common sense, and tolerance of other cultures, rather than religious doctrine, were considered to be more accurate sources of truth. New ideas about democracy and freedom led directly to both the American and French Revolutions in the late 1700s, and in the eighteenth and nineteenth centuries, medicine went through its own kind of revolution.

Science and Medicine in the Age of Reason

The new Enlightenment way of thinking about science, politics, government, and other areas of life was carried over into the arena of medicine. Physicians were beginning to write more accurate descriptions of diseases based on direct observation of patients and their symptoms, but there was still no clear, provable explanation as to what actually caused illnesses. Many physicians chose to stay with the old Hippocratic idea that illness was caused by environmental factors such as diet, exercise, and lifestyle. Others still believed in the concept of disease-causing miasmas, or "bad airs," arising from decaying animals, low swampy areas, or dirty, crowded conditions such as jails and poorhouses. Others, however, came very close to the truth by suggesting that there was something in the air, a "contagion" that got into a person and caused the disease and that could spread to others by close contact.

New ideas about the nature of disease were not leading to new methods of treatment, however, and average life

Pathology

Pathology is the study of diseased tissues in order to determine how the disease affects organs to cause symptoms and death. It was pioneered by Italian Giovanni Battista Morgagni (1682–1771). Morgagni believed that the examination of the body after death would reveal how changes in the organs were brought about by the illness that caused the death. Using information obtained from over seven hundred autopsies, Morgagni found that specific diseases affected specific organs, rather than the entire body. He described the changes in the heart after a heart attack, how a stroke affects brain tissue, and changes in the lungs from emphysema. At age eighty, he published *De sedibus et causis morborum* (On the Sites and Causes of Disease).

Other physicians followed Morgagni's work. Matthew Baillie (1761–1823) also studied emphysema, as well as cirrhosis of the liver, which he correctly blamed on alcohol abuse. He also wrote about stomach ulcers and heart disease. Frenchman Marie Francois Xavier Bichat (1771–1802) took pathology to a more precise level by asserting that disease was not so much a problem with the entire organ, but rather a problem with the tissues that made up the organ. German scientists Matthias Schleiden and Theodor Schwann took it one step further with their development of the cell theory. The work of these and other Enlightenment researchers laid the foundation for modern pathology.

Italian anatomist Giovanni Battista Morgagni believed that autopsies could reveal changes caused in the body by disease. He is considered the father of pathology.

expectancy in Europe was still under forty years. English pathologist Matthew Baillie wrote, "I know better perhaps than another man, from my knowledge of anatomy, how to discover disease, but when I have done so, I don't know better how to cure it."[36] Bloodletting was still used, especially since it was promoted by the noted American surgeon Benjamin Rush of Philadelphia. Other traditional methods involving diet, clean air, hygiene, adequate exercise and sleep, and regular bowel function were considered essential for maintaining and restoring health. The wealthy traveled to the countryside for relaxation or to spas to take in the fresh air and clean water. Others mainly treated themselves with homemade concoctions ("kitchen physic") or relied on religious or folk healers. Magic, witchcraft, and astrology were declining in a time of increasing literacy but were still sought after among the less educated.

A Medical Breakthrough

One very important development in the 1700s was the introduction of a procedure called inoculation, also called variolation. In the eighteenth century smallpox ran rampant throughout Europe, killing thousands each year. Those who survived were often left with disfiguring scars (pock marks) from blisters that covered the face and body. At this time no one knew yet about disease-causing germs or how the immune system worked. It had long been known, however, that those who survived smallpox never got it a second time. Since at least the sixteenth century, the Chinese had been using the powdered scabs of smallpox sores, inhaled through the nose, to create a mild case of smallpox from which the person would recover and then be immune to the disease in the future. Little attention was paid to this in Europe until the wealthy Englishwoman Lady Mary Wortley Montagu, while living in Constantinople, Turkey, learned about "smallpox parties" at which women would open a person's vein and insert a tiny bit of the material from the inside of a smallpox sore. The person would get a mild case but then would not be vulnerable to it again. In a letter written to a friend in 1717, she described the procedure:

The smallpox, so fatal and so general among us, is here entirely harmless by the invention of ingrafting, which is the term they give it here. There is a set of old women who make it their business to perform the operation in the month of September. . . . They make parties for the purpose, and when they are met . . . the old woman comes with a nutshell full of the matter of the best sort of smallpox, and asks what vein you will please to have opened. She immediately rips open the one that you offer to her with a large needle . . . and puts into the vein as much venom [blister contents] as can lie upon the head of her needle . . . and in this manner opens four or five veins. . . . I am very well satisfied with the safety of the experiment since I intend to try it on my dear little son.[37]

Physician Edward Jenner vaccinates a child against smallpox by inoculating the child with cowpox serum.

She was fascinated by this procedure, as her own brother had died of smallpox, and she herself had survived a case of it that left her face scarred.

Inoculation was not actually as safe as Lady Montagu believed, and people sometimes died from the milder case, but the death rate was still far less than from the more severe form that people caught naturally. British physicians became interested, and experiments were conducted, mostly using prisoners as test subjects. The procedure was improved, and physicians in Europe and America were soon inoculating hundreds of people.

Englishman Edward Jenner (1749–1823) was one of the physicians doing inoculations. Jenner was a country doctor who had observed that farm people who had had a mild disease called cowpox never got smallpox. He wondered if inoculation with cowpox matter would give a person immunity to smallpox. In May 1796 he inoculated an eight-year-old boy named James Phipps with matter taken from a cowpox sore on the arm of a local dairy maid. The boy developed a mild fever but recovered quickly. Several weeks later Jenner inoculated James with smallpox matter, but James did not get smallpox. Edward Jenner's theory proved to be correct. He called his procedure *vaccination*, from the Latin word *vacca*, meaning "cow." Jenner published his findings in 1798, and vaccination rapidly took hold. The French general Napoléon Bonaparte had his entire army vaccinated. By 1840 the more dangerous procedure of inoculation with smallpox was abandoned in favor of Edward Jenner's vaccination.

Medicine in the 1800s

By 1800 Enlightenment thinking had thoroughly penetrated into science and medicine. Medicine became more scientific, as doctors sought out rational, observable explanations for diseases and treatments based on sound science. Hospitals became not only places for the care of the poor and sick, but also institutions of medical education and research. European medical schools and research centers, especially in France and Germany, were at this time superior to American ones, and American students flocked to Europe to learn the latest information.

The 1800s was a time of rapid scientific, medical, and technical innovation and invention. Anatomy continued to gain importance as a science; *Gray's Anatomy*, considered one of the most important anatomical textbooks, was first published in 1858 and is still in print today. New diseases of the adrenal and thyroid glands, the kidneys, and the heart and blood vessels were described. New information about the chemistry of nutrition and the process of digestion was discovered. German scientists Matthias Schleiden (1804–1881) and Theodor Schwann (1820–1882) developed the cell theory—that living tissues are made up of cells, which are the basic units of plant and animal function. Rudolf Virchow (1821–1902) added that cells are formed from other cells by cell division and that disease, particularly cancer, is caused by abnormal changes in cells.

Laboratories evolved for research involving microscopy, chemistry, dissections, and experiments of all kinds, and the use of animals for experimentation became more common. Laboratory work also improved understanding of how drugs (including poisons) worked and led to the development of new drugs such as colchicine for gout, morphine and codeine for pain control, caffeine, nicotine, cocaine, and many others. The science of pharmacology became an important part of medical education.

New medical technologies appeared during the 1800s. The spirometer, invented in 1846, measured the amount of air moved with each breath. The first practical thermometer for measuring body temperature was developed in 1867, but the significance of measuring temperature was not fully understood, and patients did not trust them. Robert Morris of New York wrote, "An old Irish lady in one of our Bellevue Hospital wards would not allow a thermometer to be put in her mouth on the ground that the doctor had put it in that of a patient in the next bed who had died less than an hour afterward."[38] Blood transfusion was first performed in 1818. The electrocardiogram came in 1887. German photographer Wilhelm Röntgen discovered X-rays in 1895, and in 1896 the sphygmomanometer was introduced for measuring blood pressure. Perhaps the most useful technological invention, however, came early in the century and is still used by almost every physician every day—the stethoscope.

The Stethoscope

Since the time of the ancient Greeks, examination of the heart and lungs had been limited to listening to chest sounds by placing the ear directly to the chest (direct auscultation). This method had its limitations, however. In 1816 a young French physician named René-Théophile-Hyacinthe Laënnec found himself faced with a dilemma:

> I was consulted by a young woman laboring under general symptoms of diseased heart, and in whose case percussion and the application of the hand were of little avail on account of the great degree of fatness. The other method just mentioned [direct auscultation] being rendered inadmissible by the age and sex of the patient, I happened to recollect a simple and well-known fact in acoustics, . . . the great distinctness with which we hear the scratch of a pin at one end of a piece of wood on applying our ear to the other. Immediately, on this suggestion, I rolled a quire of paper into a kind of cylinder and applied one end of it to the region of the heart and the other to my ear, and was not a little surprised and pleased to find that I could thereby perceive the action of the heart in a manner much more clear and distinct than I had ever been able to do by the immediate application of my ear.[39]

French physician René Laënnec invented the stethoscope, which he called le cylinder, *in 1816.*

Following this initial observation, Laënnec constructed a simple tubular instrument, made of wood, approximately 9 inches (23cm) long and 1.5 inches (3.8cm) in diameter, with a hole bored through the center that widened at the end of the tube. He called it simply *le cylinder* (the cylinder). Later he chose the name *stethoscope*, from the Greek *stethos* (chest) and *skopein* (observer).

After using his stethoscope on almost three thousand patients, Laënnec described and documented many different chest sounds. He became skilled at diagnosing chest illnesses such as bronchitis, pneumonia, and tuberculosis. Initial acceptance of the new device was mixed. Some physicians feared ap-

pearing foolish, holding a long tube to their patients' chests. Others claimed that it was no more effective than placing the ear to the chest. Most physicians in Europe and America, however, saw the value of the stethoscope, and it gained favor in Europe and in America. Ironically, in 1826 Laënnec contracted and died of tuberculosis, the diagnosis made by his nephew with his own stethoscope.

Improvements to Laënnec's stethoscope and new uses for it soon followed. In 1821 Laënnec's friend Jean Alexandre Le Jumeau de Kergaradec showed how the stethoscope could be used in obstetrics for listening to the fetal heartbeat and for identifying twins.

S. Scott Allison introduced the differential (double) stethoscope in 1858. It allowed the doctor to listen to sounds from two different parts of the chest at the same time. Electric stethoscopes that amplified sounds appeared as early as 1878 and coincided with the development of the microphone and the telephone.

The Mystery of Disease

By the 1800s medical people had known for centuries that some diseases could spread from person to person, but they did not know how it happened. Girolamo Fracastoro had written about "disease seeds" as early as 1546. In 1683 Antoni van Leeuwenhoek observed microbes—microscopic organisms such as yeasts, protozoa, and bacteria—under his microscope and called them "animalcules." Others had observed that bacteria would appear in containers of broth even if the container had been sealed shut. Microbes were also observed

Florence Nightingale

At the beginning of the nineteenth century, nurses in the public hospitals were generally untrained, illiterate girls and women who were sometimes criminals or alcoholics. Nursing was considered an entirely unsuitable pursuit for respectable women. In the 1800s reformers sought to improve hospital conditions in several ways, including improving nursing care.

In England the cause of better nursing was taken up by Florence Nightingale (1820–1910), a young woman from a wealthy family who claimed to have had a vision directing her to serve mankind. Trained at a school in Germany, she quickly gained an excellent reputation. In 1854, when the British became involved in the Crimean War, she responded to reports of the deplorable conditions of the military medical facilities there and took a group of thirty-eight nurses to Scutari, Turkey. A firm miasmatist (a believer in "bad air" as the cause of disease), she never accepted the germ theory but transformed the hospital with cleanliness, fresh air, light, and better food. The death rate plummeted from about 40 percent to about 2 percent in six months.

Upon her return to England, she devoted herself to making nursing a respectable skilled profession. She opened schools that stressed scientific nursing theory and practice and accepted students from all classes of society. She also trained teachers and administrators for her schools. The Nightingale system of nursing education spread to other European countries, as well as Australia, Scandinavia, and America.

in rotting plant and animal material and in fermented substances such as alcohol and soured milk.

No one could explain where these "little animals" came from. Some believed that they were created out of the material in which they grew—the idea of "spontaneous generation." There was no reason to think that they were the very "disease seeds" that caused illness or that each particular kind of microbe caused a specific disease. The origin of microbes and their relationship with disease became much clearer, however, with the work of Louis Pasteur and Robert Koch.

Louis Pasteur

Louis Pasteur (1822–1896), the son of a tanner, went to Paris to study chemistry and biology. He became interested in the process of fermentation—how it soured milk and how it created vinegar and the alcohol in wine and beer. At that time fermentation was thought to be a chemical process, but by 1860 Pasteur had discovered that it was actually biological, the result of living organisms such as yeasts. Pasteur went on to perform experiments that proved that microbes existed in the air, disproving the idea of spontaneous generation. He also showed that they were responsible for decomposition of plant and animal material (putrefaction). His discovery that microbes could be killed with heat led to the process of pasteurization, which revolutionized food safety by providing a way to kill disease-causing organisms in food, especially milk. Another important

experiment showed that the silkworm disease pebrine was caused by a particular kind of protozoan.

After these and other experiments, Pasteur concluded that fermentation, putrefaction, and disease were all caused by living microorganisms that existed in the environment and that specific organisms caused specific diseases. He theorized that by identifying the organisms, vaccines like Edward Jenner's could be made that would prevent people from getting the diseases they caused.

Pasteur set out to test his theories with two diseases, chicken cholera and bovine (cow) anthrax. In separate experiments, he prepared vaccines using attenuated, or weakened, versions of the cholera and anthrax organisms and vaccinated a group of test animals. A control group of animals received no vaccine. He then injected all the animals with live organisms. All of the unvaccinated chickens got cholera, and the unvaccinated cows got anthrax, but none of the vaccinated animals got sick. His experiments were a success. It was with another disease, however, that Pasteur solidified his place in medical history—the dreaded, and always fatal, rabies.

Louis Pasteur and Rabies

In the nineteenth century rabies was a greatly feared disease because of its terrible and painful symptoms and because it always caused death. In 1546 Italian physician Girolamo Fracastoro of Verona had written one of the first-known informational writings dealing

French chemist and microbiologist Louis Pasteur discovered that fermentation, putrefaction, and disease were caused by specific microorganisms. He created vaccines for cholera and anthrax in 1880.

exclusively with infectious disease, in which he described the symptoms of rabies in great detail, calling it "the incurable wound." He wrote:

> The patient can neither stand nor lie down; like a mad man he flings himself hither and thither, tears his flesh with his hands, and feels intolerable thirst. This is the most distressing symptom, for he so shrinks from water and all liquids that he would rather die than drink or be brought near to water. It is then they bite other persons, foam at the mouth, their eyes look twisted, and finally they are exhausted and painfully breathe their last.[40]

In 1804 German scientist Georg Gottfried Zinke confirmed that rabies was transmitted by the bite of an infected animal through its saliva. In 1879 an important discovery was made when Pierre Galtier, a veterinarian, found that transmitting the disease through a series of rabbits would eventually weaken, or attenuate, the organism that caused rabies.

In 1880, having succeeded with chicken cholera and anthrax vaccines, Louis Pasteur took on rabies as his next target. He was unable to identify the problematic organism this time, however, because rabies is caused by a virus, which is many times smaller than bacteria and not visible with an ordinary microscope. He proceeded with experiments anyway, using ground-up spinal cord tissue from infected rabbits. Building on Galtier's work, he attenuated the virus by passing it through a series of rabbits. He then injected the weakened material into healthy dogs. Over fourteen days, he injected increasingly more virulent, or stronger, versions of the virus and found that the dogs did not get rabies even when they received the most virulent material injected directly into their brains.

Pasteur felt it was time to test the vaccine on a person, but test subjects were hard to find because of the frightening nature of the disease. He considered infecting himself with rabies, but it turned out to be unnecessary. Like Edward Jenner a century earlier, Pasteur was unexpectedly presented with his opportunity. In July 1885 nine-year-old Josef Meister was brought to Pasteur after being bitten fourteen times by a rabid dog. Pasteur was anxious about trying his vaccine on a child, but he knew that the boy would certainly die without it. That evening he gave Josef the first of thirteen increasingly virulent injections, given over ten days. On the tenth day, Josef returned home with no signs of rabies. Another success came three months later when Pasteur treated a young shepherd boy. Over the next year and a half, almost two thousand patients were treated with the vaccine.

The vaccine was not perfect, and some treated patients still died from rabies or suffered permanent side effects. Pasteur was openly criticized for his work, but he continued, and results improved. In 1886 only one person died of rabies in Paris, compared to about twelve per year over the previous five years. In 1888 the Pasteur Institute was founded, mainly for rabies research. When he grew up,

The Golden Age of Quackery

The age of reason was a time of increasing literacy and improving economic resources among the general public, especially in America. People were eager to exercise their own judgments and make their own decisions about their health. Mass production of books about health, such as *The Poor Man's Medicine Chest* (1791), brought medical knowledge to the masses, and there was a demand for new and different healing methods. The environment was ripe for the emergence of quacks, people (many of them physicians) who traveled from town to town selling all sorts of false "medicines" that they claimed would cure almost anything. The medicines had attractive names such as Solomon's Balm of Gilead, Dr. Kilmer's Swamp Root, or Mug-Wump Specific. Many of these, called patent medicines, were made mostly of alcohol, such as Dr. Hostettler's Stomach Bitters, which at 44 percent alcohol was more potent than whiskey. Others, including preparations made for babies and children, contained drugs such as cocaine or opium, which did nothing to actually treat the person and could lead to addiction. Some quacks sold inventions, such as Scotsman James Craham, who claimed that his Celestial Bed would lengthen life. Others charged for their own special treatments such as mud baths, hypnotism, or "animal magnetism."

Eventually, efforts to control quackery appeared in most countries. In the United States journalists published newspaper articles exposing the dangers of patent medicines. In France the Royal Society of Medicine claimed the right to examine the contents of patent medicines. In contrast, England took the hands-off attitude of caveat emptor, a Latin phrase meaning "let the buyer beware."

Josef Meister became the doorman for the institute.

Robert Koch

Whereas Louis Pasteur had focused his attention on creating vaccines for diseases, Robert Koch (1843–1910) turned his attention to identifying particular organisms with certain diseases. If a particular organism were shown to be responsible for causing a disease, then that would be the first step toward controlling that disease.

His first great success with this came in 1882, when he discovered the bacterium which causes tuberculosis. In 1883 he went to Egypt, then to India the following year, to investigate outbreaks of cholera in those countries, and he was able to identify that bacterium, too.

Later Koch returned to his work on tuberculosis but was unable to develop an effective vaccine for the illness. Meanwhile, other researchers used methods he pioneered to develop a very effective

German bacteriologist Robert Koch developed a set of criteria—known as Koch's postulates—for judging whether a given organism causes a given disease. He won the Nobel Prize for his work in 1905.

vaccine for the often fatal disease diphtheria. His methods were used in the following years to identify the organisms responsible for syphilis, typhoid, plague, pneumonia, meningitis, leprosy, tetanus, whooping cough, and other bacterial infections.

Robert Koch is also known for devising a set of conditions that must be met in order to prove that a particular germ causes a particular illness. These conditions came to be known as Koch's postulates:

- The organism must be present in every victim of the illness.
- Once removed from the body, the organism must be shown to grow and reproduce itself in laboratory conditions.
- It must be shown that the cultured (lab-grown) organisms cause the same disease when injected into a test animal.
- The organism must then be removed from the test animal and a new culture made from it.

If all four of these conditions were met, the organism was thereby proved to be the one responsible for the illness. For his work Robert Koch won the Nobel Prize for Medicine in 1905.

Surgery and Sepsis

Until the late 1800s one of the most significant dangers involved with having surgery was the high risk of infection in the surgical incision, or cut. If an infection gets into the blood, it travels to all parts of the body and can quickly overwhelm the body's natural defenses, a condition called sepsis. Death from sepsis was a common occurrence, but with no knowledge of disease-causing germs, there was little the doctors could do to prevent it. Since ancient times certain substances such as wine, vinegar, mercury, and iodine were known to help decrease the chances of infection, but none of them was very effective in preventing surgical infections.

Sepsis and death from infection after giving birth, called puerperal fever, was also extremely common at this time, especially in women who had given birth in a hospital rather than at home. In the mid-1840s Viennese physician Ignaz Semmelweis noticed that new mothers who had been attended by a doctor or medical student were far more likely to get puerperal fever than those who were attended by midwives. He suspected that the reason for this was that doctors often came directly from doing autopsies (examining dead bodies) to delivering babies, without washing their hands or their instruments. He concluded that the fever was caused by "putrid particles," carried from the autopsy to the new mothers on the hands of the physicians. He ordered both doctors and midwives to wash their hands with chlorinated lime water before deliveries. As a result, the death rate from puerperal fever fell from as much as 30 percent to less than 2 percent.

Following the work of Pasteur, Koch, and Semmelweis, English surgeon Joseph Lister (1827–1912) applied the new knowledge to surgery. As a surgeon in

Glasgow, Scotland, Lister was very concerned with the high rate of infection and sepsis in the hospital there. Thanks to Pasteur, Lister understood that infection was caused by microbes in the air and that chemical solutions could slow down their growth. He also knew that a chemical called carbolic acid (today called phenol) was effective in deodorizing rotting sewage. He tried using carbolic acid to clean wounds and applied dressings soaked with it. There was a sharp drop in infections and sepsis. He then had other surgeons rinse their hands with it before and after operations and had it sprayed into the air during operations.

Despite his remarkable results, many surgeons criticized Lister and denied that his techniques had anything to do with decreasing sepsis. Many still did not believe in the existence of microbes or would not admit that their own practices were at fault for causing sepsis. As the germ theory took hold, however, his techniques became more widely used in Europe and North America.

By the end of the century, the concept of antisepsis in the operating room had taken hold, and new methods to achieve it included using steam to sterilize instruments and wearing gowns, masks, and rubber gloves during surgery. Surgical antisepsis became the standard of care, and surgery became a much safer alternative for patients.

Anesthesia

Antisepsis revolutionized surgery by making it much safer. Surgery was also transformed in the nineteenth century by the development of effective anesthetics. Until then doctors could only try to deaden the pain of surgery with medications such as opium or alcohol. Surgery was an agonizing experience for the patient, and operations in the chest or abdomen were almost impossible. In 1811 novelist Fanny Burney wrote a long account describing in chilling detail her experience having a mastectomy (the removal of a breast): "When the dreadful steel was plunged into the breast—cutting through veins—arteries—flesh—nerves— . . . I began a scream that lasted . . . during the whole time of the incision —& I almost marvel that it rings not in my Ears still! So excruciating was the agony."[41]

In 1772 the gaseous substance nitrous oxide had been developed as a treatment for tuberculosis. In 1800 British chemist Humphrey Davy discovered that the gas created a feeling of giddiness and dizziness, that it could relieve pain, and when mixed with oxygen, would cause unconsciousness. He suggested then that it may have a use in surgery, but instead it became only a popular form of entertainment at "laughing gas parties."

In 1842 William Clark removed an infected tooth using ether, a liquid chemical that had first been created in 1540. The ether was dripped onto a cloth, which was placed over the patient's nose and mouth. Breathing the fumes caused unconsciousness. Two months later, Crawford Long used ether to remove a mass from a boy's neck. Both operations were done without pain. The use of ether for surgery quickly spread to Europe, and it was used on the battlefield during the Crimean War (1853–56).

Ether had its disadvantages. It was highly flammable, was irritating to the lungs, and caused nausea and vomiting after surgery. It was eventually replaced with another liquid chemical called chloroform, discovered in 1831. In 1853 Queen Victoria of England was given chloroform during the birth of her son Prince Leopold. For minor operations that did not need complete unconsciousness, the drug cocaine was synthesized from coca leaves in 1885. Until 1903 cocaine was an ingredient in the soft drink Coca-Cola, which was first created as a medicine for various ailments.

Thanks to the revolutionary work of Louis Pasteur, Robert Koch, and others, doctors now had a much clearer idea of what caused major diseases. This knowledge opened the door to new ways to prevent, treat, and cure those diseases. The next century saw an explosion in safe, effective medical care.

Chapter Six

Challenges in the Twentieth Century and Beyond

As the twentieth century dawned, discoveries made in the new science of bacteriology—the study of microscopic organisms—led to a steep decline in the number of illnesses and deaths from microbes. New vaccines prevented suffering from many of the world's fatal diseases. Antisepsis made surgery a safer option for treatment. In the early part of the century, research into the human immune system opened the door to new ways to fight infection.

Unlocking the Secret of Immunity

The work of Louis Pasteur, Robert Koch, and others had resulted in the development of vaccines that provided immunity to a wide array of diseases. What was still not understood, however, was exactly how these vaccines created immunity in the vaccinated person or how the body developed a natural immunity on its own after having a disease. In 1884 Russian scientist Ilya Metchnikoff (1845–1916) observed cells in the blood that seemed to ingest, or eat, disease germs. He called these cells phagocytes. He also noticed that the body made many more phagocytes whenever an infection was present. These discoveries developed into one theory of immunity called the cellular theory.

Meanwhile, German scientists such as Paul Ehrlich (1854–1915) were focusing their attention on more molecular theories of immunity, which focused on chemical explanations rather than biological ones. Ehrlich proposed that toxins, or poisons, produced by germs caused disease by attaching themselves to what he called "side chains" on body cells. This would interfere with the cells' function enough to cause the disease symptoms. In response to the toxin, the cell would produce new side

92 ■ The History of Medicine

chains. These new side chains came to be called antibodies.

Ehrlich theorized that the antibodies would break off the cell and remain permanently in the body after recovery from the disease. If the person were to become exposed to that disease again, the antibodies would bind to the toxin so that it could not bind to the body's cells. In this way the person would not become ill a second time. Ehrlich and others became very interested in developing drugs that could mimic bacterial toxins and stimulate the body to produce antibodies to them. In a 1906 speech Ehrlich proposed selective medicines that would "be able to exert their full action exclusively on the parasite harbored within the organism and would represent, so to speak, magic bullets which seek their target of their own accord."[42]

The First Antibiotics

Paul Ehrlich's first target was the sexually transmitted disease (STD) syphilis, which was very easily spread between people and killed thousands. The organism responsible had been found in 1905, and a blood test for it had been

German bacteriologist Paul Ehrlich is pictured in his laboratory testing the drug that would make syphilis a curable disease. As a result of his work, he became a joint winner of the 1908 Nobel Prize for Medicine.

developed the following year. Treatment still relied on dangerous compounds made from mercury or arsenic. Ehrlich created and tested over six hundred different compounds using arsenic and discovered that one of them, named salvarsan, was especially effective. Although it still had side effects, it was a major improvement over mercury.

Other researchers took on other diseases. In 1932 Gerhard Domagk (1895–1964) discovered that a chemical dye called Prontosil red could cure mice infected with streptococcus, a common bacterium that causes diseases such as scarlet fever, tonsillitis, and erysipelas, a skin infection. A related compound was found to be effective against pneumococcus, a bacterium that can cause pneumonia, meningitis, and ear infections. Both drugs, eventually called sulfa drugs, also showed effectiveness against puerperal fever, urinary tract infections, and the STD gonorrhea. By the 1940s sulfa drugs were being used widely and were sent with soldiers into battle in World War II to prevent and treat infections in wounds.

While Ehrlich, Domagk, and others were developing chemical agents for fighting infections, others were looking into biological methods. Pasteur and others had already noted that some kinds of bacteria could halt the growth of other kinds. They called these "killer" bacteria antibiotes, meaning "destructive of life." Eventually the word *antibiotic* came into use. One of today's most effective and widely used antibiotics was discovered as a result of a laboratory accident.

Alexander Fleming and Penicillin

Scottish bacteriologist Alexander Fleming (1888–1955) was one of those looking for biological alternatives to the harsh chemical antiseptics that were being used to cleanse battle wounds during World War I. In 1928 he was studying a common skin bacterium called staphylococcus (or staph) and had several culture dishes of the organism in his laboratory. After being gone for a while on vacation, he returned to his lab to discover that one of his culture dishes had been left open and had been contaminated with some kind of mold. He noticed immediately that the staph cultures near the mold had been destroyed, while those farther away in the dish were still intact. He identified the mold as a member of the genus *Penicillium* and gave the name *penicillin* to the bacteria-killing substance it produced. Fleming set out to see what other organisms penicillin might be used against.

Penicillin proved to be highly effective against several, but not all, kinds of bacteria. It was also difficult to produce in large quantities. Because of these problems, Fleming decided not to pursue its development as an antibiotic. Other scientists, however, took on the challenge and developed improved methods for isolating penicillin from the mold. By 1943, at the height of World War II, British and American drug companies were mass-producing enough penicillin to treat every wounded soldier. It not only worked to prevent wound infections, it also cured pneumonia, gonor-

The Evolution of Anesthesia

Early anesthetics such as ether put patients to sleep, but there were serious drawbacks. Dosages could not be regulated, and patients might wake up during surgery or might not wake up at all. They could be highly flammable, and they had unpleasant and dangerous side effects. Injectable anesthetic drugs such as sodium pentothal (nicknamed "truth serum" for its supposed ability to make people reveal secrets while under its influence) were introduced in the 1930s so dosages could be controlled, but side effects remained, and it was not fully understood exactly how they worked. Other anesthetic gases such as halothane, isoflurane, and enflurane were developed in the 1950s and were much safer than ether.

Today doctors understand that anesthesia has several components besides just unconsciousness, including sedation ("twilight sleep"), analgesia (painlessness), muscle paralysis, and amnesia (no memory of events during anesthesia). Some minor procedures can be done under local anesthesia, in which the specific part to be operated on is numbed with an injection of an anesthetic medication. Others can be done using regional anesthesia, such as spinal anesthesia, in which a larger area of the body is anesthetized. Sophisticated monitoring devices and a variety of other types of medications help the anesthesia provider maintain the patient's blood pressure, heart function, blood oxygen level, and level of unconsciousness within safe limits. Modern anesthetics have fewer side effects, and anesthesia providers are highly trained and skilled medical doctors and nurses, making anesthesia safe and effective for the patient.

rhea, meningitis, anthrax, syphilis, diphtheria, and tetanus.

In 1945 Fleming and two others received the Nobel Prize for their work on penicillin. Years later Fleming said of his accidental discovery:

I have been trying to point out that in our lives chance may have an astonishing influence and, if I may offer advice to the young laboratory worker, it would be this—never to neglect an extraordinary appearance or happening. It may be—usually is, in fact—a false alarm that leads to nothing, but it may on the other hand be the clue provided by fate to lead you to some important advance.[43]

The Discovery of Viruses

Following the development of penicillin, the race was on to discover and develop more antibiotics that would work on more infections. In 1940 an antibiotic substance called actinomycin (used today only in cancer treatment) was isolated form a soil bacterium. This was followed by streptomycin, for tuberculosis and plague, in 1944 and isoniazid, also for tuberculosis, in 1950. None of the new antibiotics, however, was effective against diseases that were caused by viruses.

Viral diseases had been a mystery for centuries. With the development of the germ theory in the late 1800s, scientists searched for the organisms that caused diseases such as yellow fever, measles, and polio so that vaccines could be developed, as they had been for smallpox and rabies. After 1918, when a worldwide outbreak of influenza killed as many as 100 million people, there was enormous pressure on the scientific and medical communities to come up with an effective influenza vaccine.

The problem that kept researchers from developing vaccines for diseases like influenza was that no bacteria could be seen in samples taken from victims of those diseases. Special filters called Chamberland filters were used that could separate bacteria out of liquids, but the filtered liquid from these diseases could still cause the disease even though there were no bacteria in it. Scientists believed that the filtered fluid itself must be toxic, and the name "filterable virus" (*virus* from the Latin word for "poison") was used to refer to the fluid.

An important advance came in 1935 when, while studying a plant disease called tobacco mosaic virus, American biochemist Wendell Stanley discovered that viruses were not liquids but were actually particles made of protein. In 1937 Thomas Francis began to explore the possibility of creating a vaccine for influenza by using viral cultures. By 1943 he had developed a flu vaccine from killed flu virus that worked the same way bacterial vaccines worked. It was given to American soldiers during World War II. That same year scientists were finally able to see the elusive virus with the invention of the electron microscope.

In the next twenty years, vaccines were developed for mumps (1949), polio (1955), and measles (1963). In 1980, following a global vaccination effort begun in 1958, the World Health Organization (WHO) declared that smallpox, once one of the deadliest viral diseases known to man, had been eradicated— eliminated from the earth. The crippling disease polio is the next target for eradication; according to the Global Eradication Initiative, in 2011 there were only 364 cases reported globally as of September, compared to 641 in 2010 and 1,349 in 2009. A year after smallpox was declared gone from the earth, a brand-new virus appeared that causes one of the most feared diseases in history—acquired immune deficiency syndrome, or AIDS.

The AIDS Pandemic

In the late 1970s and early 1980s, doctors in California and New York began noticing an unusual rise in the occurrence of a rare kind of pneumonia, called pneumocystis carinii, and a rare skin cancer called Kaposi's sarcoma, among gay men. These diseases were opportunistic, meaning they were most common in people with inadequate immune systems. Concern arose that a new disease had appeared, and the Centers for Disease Control and Prevention in Atlanta, Georgia, began an investigation. By the end of 1981, the illness, now called acquired immune deficiency syndrome, or AIDS, began to appear in heterosexual people, drug addicts, and people who had received blood transfusions.

In 1983 researchers at the Pasteur Institute in Paris identified a virus in the blood of AIDS patients that they named human immunodeficiency virus, or HIV. Researchers scrambled to find some kind of treatment for the deadly new virus. By this time AIDS had appeared in thirty-three countries, spreading especially fast in African countries. By the next year there were eight thousand cases of AIDS in the United States,

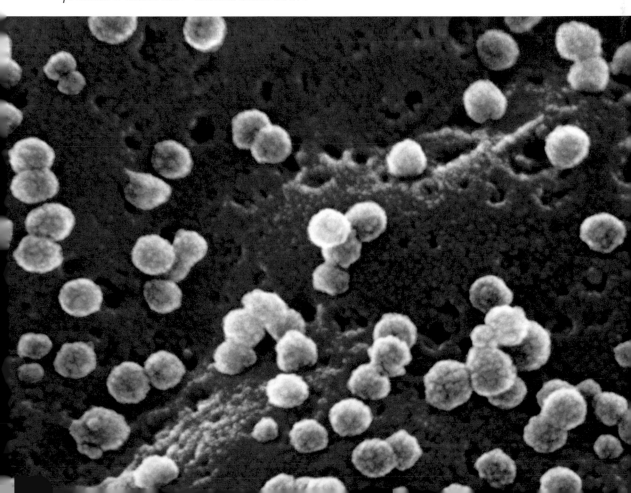

Shown here is an electron micrograph of the insidious human immunodeficiency virus (HIV), which attacks the human immune system. Scientists have been attempting to produce a viable HIV vaccine since 1987.

with over thirty-seven hundred deaths. Massive public education programs were begun in an effort to slow the spread of the virus.

Finally, in 1987 a drug called Retrovir was introduced to treat AIDS, but by 1990 the number of known cases rose to 1 million worldwide. In 1992 a new drug called Hivid was introduced to be used in combination with Retrovir. In 1996 a new class of drugs called protease inhibitors was developed. When used in combination, the drugs were effective in controlling the progression of the disease and delaying death, but those infected with HIV still could not be cured. Twenty years after the first cases appeared, over 31 million people were living with HIV. During the early 2000s, more drugs were introduced, but by 2005 the number of infected people grew to about 40 million, with 25 million total deaths, and cases had been reported in every country in the world. In 2009 the entire genome, the complete genetic profile, of HIV was mapped, raising hope for an effective vaccine. According to the UNAIDS, the United Nations organization leading the international campaign against AIDS, there were 2.6 million new cases of AIDS reported in 2009, down from 3.1 million in 2001.

Surgery in the Twentieth Century

Surgery is another area of medicine that saw profound improvement in the twentieth century. Antiseptic practices and anesthesia brought surgery into the modern age, making it safer and less painful. New surgical procedures were developed, especially for problems in the chest, abdomen, and brain. Doctors began to specialize, becoming more proficient in specific types of surgery, and surgery became a first-line treatment rather than a last resort. By 1925 removing the tonsils (tonsillectomy) had become the most common surgical procedure, being performed on thousands of children in America and Europe each year. Operations to remove the appendix (appendectomy), the gallbladder (cholecystectomy), and the uterus (hysterectomy) also became more common by the 1920s.

Two areas of the body that had always been inaccessible to the surgeon until the late 1800s were the brain and the heart. With the exception of trepanning, no one had been inside the head until 1879, when William Macewan successfully removed a brain tumor. In the United States, the leader in brain surgery was Harvey Cushing (1869–1939). Cushing removed thousands of brain tumors during his career, with a mortality rate of only about 8 percent. His work made neurosurgery a viable treatment option.

In 1896 Stephen Paget wrote that "surgery of the heart has probably reached the limits set by Nature to all surgery; no new method, and no new discovery, can overcome the natural difficulties that attend a wound of the heart."[44] In the twentieth century, however, new discoveries in cardiovascular (heart and blood vessel) disease did just that. In 1910 Alexis Carrell devised a way to sew blood vessels together to bypass blocked arteries or repair damaged vessels. In the 1930s cardiac catheterization was developed, which involves threading a very thin tube (catheter) into the heart through a vein in the arm or leg, injecting a special dye, and taking X-rays to show the inner workings of the heart. The heart-lung machine (now called a perfusion machine), which takes over the function of the heart and lungs during open heart surgery, was perfected in the 1950s, and in the late 1960s coronary artery bypass grafts (CABG) for blocked heart arteries were begun. In this operation pieces of vein, usually taken from the leg, are used to reroute blood around the blocked part of the artery. Today the CABG is the most commonly performed heart surgery in the United States, with over one hundred thousand being performed each year.

Minimally Invasive Surgery

Minimally invasive surgery is a way of performing a surgical procedure through several very small incisions, usually about 0.25 inches to 0.75 inches (0.5cm –1.5cm) long, rather than one large one. The most common kind of minimally invasive surgery, called laparoscopic surgery, involves using a long, narrow lens, called a laparoscope, to look into the abdomen. The laparoscope is connected to a light source, which shines light through the laparoscope into the abdomen, and to a special camera that sends a video signal to a monitor that

looks like a television screen. The laparoscope is inserted into the abdomen through a plastic tube called a port. Other small incisions are made, through which long, narrow instruments are inserted through their own ports. The surgeon uses the instruments to do the surgery while watching the procedure on the monitor.

The first laparoscopic procedure was performed in 1910. At first it was mainly used by gynecologists to diagnose problems in the female pelvis. There was no camera; the surgeon would look directly into the laparoscope through an eyepiece. Improvements in laparoscopic technique and equipment were made over the following decades, and in 1983 German surgeon Kurt Semm performed an appendectomy using laparoscopy. Two years later another German, Erich Muhe, performed a laparoscopic cholecystectomy. In 1982 the laparoscopic camera was added, which allowed projection of the image onto the monitor screen. The quality and resolution of the image was greatly improved in the late 1980s with the addition of a computer chip in the camera. With these improvements, laparoscopy was embraced by general surgeons as well.

Today almost all abdominal and pelvic operations can be performed using a laparoscope, including 98 percent of all cholecystectomies. Procedures on the stomach, kidneys, liver, spleen, bowel, and other organs can also be done this way. Laparoscopic surgery has several important advantages. It causes much less damage to the tissues

Organ Transplantation

Thanks to increasing knowledge about the human immune system, organ transplantation became a reality in the twentieth century. In animal experiments doctors learned that transplanted tissues were often rejected by the host, or receiving, animal because the host's body treated the foreign tissue as if it were a disease organism. In the 1950s drugs that suppressed the immune response (immunosuppressives) were used. In 1954 the first successful kidney transplant was performed. The new kidney was donated by the patient's twin brother, whose tissues were an identical match to the patient's, and the new kidney was not rejected. Over the next twenty years, immunosuppressive drugs were improved, opening the way for transplants of other organs such as the liver, pancreas, and lungs. In 1967 the first heart transplant was performed by South African surgeon Christiaan Barnard. The introduction of the immunosuppressive drug cyclosporine in the 1970s made organ transplantation much safer, and according to Donate Life America, 28,663 organs, including hearts, livers, lungs, pancreases, livers, and intestines, were transplanted in 2010 in the United States. In addition, tissues such as skin, bone, tendons, heart valves, blood vessels, and the cornea of the eye can also be transplanted.

Heart surgeon Christiaan Barnard, assisted by his surgical team, performs the first successful heart transplant in December 1967.

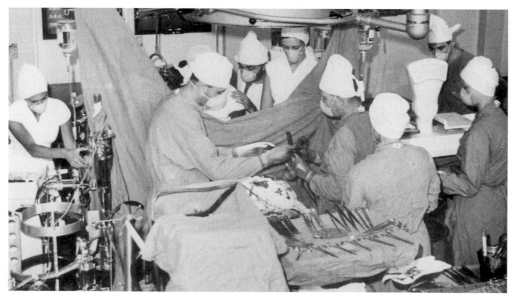

than traditional "open" surgery. There is less blood loss, less pain, a shorter hospital stay, and a shorter recovery time. Scopes of different sizes and lengths can also be used in the joints (arthroscopy), the brain, and the sinus cavities.

Robotic Surgery

In the 1950s the technology of robotics was developed, in which programmable machines are created that can mimic human movements to perform tasks. The first industrial use of robotics occurred in the early 1960s. In 1985 robotic surgery was introduced for laparoscopic procedures. In robotic surgery a robotic arm is used to hold the camera in place while the surgeon manipulates the laparoscopic instruments from a remote computer console. The robotic system senses the surgeon's hand movements in the console and transmits them electronically to other robotic arms that hold the instruments and move them smoothly and very precisely. The surgeon watches the movements of the instruments on a monitor through a pair of eyepieces, similar to some video games.

Craig Block, who uses robotics for prostate surgery, explains:

> People were doing regular laparoscopic surgery, where they make small incisions and use ports and small external tools to do internal surgery for all sorts of things. The hard part about standard laparoscopy is that it is two-dimensional. So you look at a TV screen and you lose your depth perception. And it's

also harder to run those tools because of the way they move. It's kind of like operating with chopsticks.[45]

Robotics, on the other hand, uses high-definition and 3-D technology. Another unique feature of robotics is that the signals from the console can be sent anywhere electronically, so a surgeon can actually perform procedures, including heart surgeries, on a patient in another country.

Genetics and Gene Therapy

Another area of research that saw enormous strides in the twentieth century is the field of genetics. Genetics is the study of how characteristics are transmitted from parent to offspring through their genes. Genes are microscopic structures made of a long molecule called deoxyribonucleic acid (DNA). Genes are arranged in a particular order along larger (but still microscopic) structures called chromosomes, which are located in the nucleus of every living cell. Genes carry a genetic code, or information that determines how a particular organism will look, behave, and function. Every organism has a particular set of genes—its genome—which is unique to that kind of organism. One of the most significant technological advances in science and medicine of the twentieth century was discovering how individual genes affect individual characteristics. This led to learning how to modify and use genes to change their effect in the organism.

The study of genetics actually began in the late 1800s with the work of a

Austrian botanist and Catholic friar Gregor Mendel's work on heredity in the flowers of the common pea became the basis from which modern genetic theory would evolve.

Catholic friar named Gregor Mendel. He discovered that the colors of pea flowers varied depending on what color the "parent" plants were. Later, scientists confirmed and added to Mendel's work, and by the early twentieth century, Mendelian genetics had been applied to many plants and animals.

In the 1950s the molecular structure of DNA was described, and the number of human chromosomes was found to be forty-six. Over the next several decades, scientists learned how the chromosomes divide and get passed on from parent to offspring. They also learned how to determine the sequence of genes along the chromosomes, and in 2003, with the completion of the Human Genome Project, the entire sequence of human genes was mapped. Scientists could then discover which particular genes were responsible for causing genetic diseases such as sickle-cell disease, hemophilia, cystic fibrosis, Down syndrome, and others.

With the discovery of how genes work, scientists were able to devise ways to alter an individual's genetic makeup to change the way his or her genes function. This process, called genetic engineering, started in the 1970s using genes in bacteria and mice. There are many uses for genetic engineering in many fields of science, agriculture, and medicine. For example, scientists can insert genes into bacteria that will cause the bacteria to produce drugs such as insulin, necessary for people with diabetes, and human growth hormone for people with genetic growth disorders.

Another advancement in this area is gene therapy, a treatment method that uses genetic engineering technology to correct defective gene functioning. It can be done in several ways. The most common method is by replacing defective genes with healthy ones so that the cells will reproduce with the healthy gene instead of the abnormal one. Actively functioning genes can be inserted into the cell to replace genes that are not functioning. An abnormal gene can be repaired so that it resumes its normal function. An overactive or malfunctioning gene can be "turned off," or an underactive gene can be "turned up."

Gene therapy is still in its infancy and is considered an experimental treatment. More research is needed to make it a safer and more effective treatment option for people. Research is ongoing in ways to use gene therapy for a number of health issues such as sickle-cell disease, cystic fibrosis, diabetes, Alzheimer's disease, immune system disorders, and Parkinson's disease. One of the most active areas in which genetics and gene therapy are being studied is cancer research.

Cancer Treatment

Cancer is a disease characterized by rapid, uncontrolled growth of abnormal cells in a particular organ. Normally, abnormal cells die off, but in cancer, the abnormal cells continue to grow and multiply. Eventually, they replace so many healthy cells that the organ cannot carry out its function in the body. Cancerous cells can spread out of the organ in which they originated and start to grow in other parts of the body, a process called metastasis. Metastatic cancer can result in death.

Cancer has been known since ancient times. It has been one of the most feared diseases in human history because it was so hard to treat and almost impossible to cure. The improvement of surgery in the late nineteenth and early twentieth centuries gave rise to cancer operations such as Halsted's radical mastectomy, but because the nature of the disease and its causes were still unknown, effective nonsurgical treatment was not available. In the twentieth century several very important facts about cancer were learned that revolutionized cancer treatment.

Finding the Cause

In 1909 German immunologist Paul Ehrlich proposed the idea that the immune system may have a role in the formation and spread of cancer. The following year it was discovered that certain viruses could start the growth of cancerous cells. Scientists wondered if a vaccine could be developed that would help prevent cancer. The difficulty in developing cancer vaccines, however, lay in the fact that cancer cells are the body's own cells, rather than foreign cells like viruses or bacteria. As such they vary from person to person, making a vaccine that would work for everyone more difficult to develop. Another challenge was finding a drug strong enough to kill cancer cells without hurting normal cells. In 2006 the first vaccine for prevention of cancer was introduced. The vaccine targets a virus called human papillomavirus, which can cause cervical cancer in women. In April 2010 the U.S. Food and Drug Administration approved a vaccine that can treat existing prostate cancer in men.

In 1915 the relationship between hormones and cancer was discovered, particularly the relationship between the female hormone estrogen and breast cancer. In the 1970s researchers discovered that some breast cancers respond to treatment with hormone therapy, and hormone-based drugs such as Tamoxifen were developed that can be very effective in cancer treatment.

In the 1950s a genetic component of cancer was suggested when it was found that cigarette smoke is carcinogenic, or cancer causing, because it can cause mutations, or changes, in the genes of body cells that cause the cells to become cancerous. Since then research studies have shown that many substances in the modern environment, such as X-rays, artificial food additives, fertilizers, and pesticides, can cause such mutations. In the 1970s another genetic factor was discovered when scientists found that certain genes called oncogenes, when inherited from a parent, make a person more likely to get a particular kind of cancer in his or her lifetime. Many anticancer drugs target the DNA of these oncogenes to slow their activity. This allows treatment to be more tailored to the individual patient. Eran Andrechek of Michigan State University says, "With personalized medicine, we can use predictions of how genes will interact, and based on that we can make better use of existing treatments that will have more of an impact. We want to examine how we can design therapies for specific tumor types by combining genomics and current medicines. We feel this holds great promise for personalized cancer therapy."[46]

The 1980s and 1990s brought to light more information about genetics and cancer. Today people with a strong family history of certain cancers can be tested to see if they carry the genes that increase their likelihood of getting that

Stem Cell Therapy

Stem cells are cells that have the ability to differentiate, or become specialized, into other kinds of tissue or organ cells, such as a muscle cells, skin cells, or red blood cells. They can divide themselves over and over again and replace worn-out or damaged cells in organs such as the stomach and tissues such as bone marrow. Stem cells can be found in adult tissues such as bone marrow or blood, blood from an infant's umbilical cord, or amniotic fluid (which surrounds and cushions the unborn fetus in the womb). The most useful kind of stem cells, however, is embryonic stem cells, obtained from the fetus in the earliest stages of its development. For this reason stem cell research is very controversial.

Scientists study stem cells to learn more about human development and how stem cells differentiate into functioning organ and tissue cells and to learn more about the role of genes in diseases like cancer or diabetes. Stem cells that have been differentiated in the lab can be used to test new drugs such as cancer drugs. One of the most important areas of stem cell research involves cell-based therapies using stem cells to replace abnormal or damaged cells to treat human disease and other health issues. For example, stem cells could be turned into insulin-producing cells to replace abnormal pancreas cells in people with diabetes. They may be used to repair a damaged heart or liver. They can be used to regenerate nerve tissue in people who have had crippling spinal cord injuries. They can even be used to grow new organs and tissues, such as bladders, skin, bone, ear cartilage, blood vessels, and others, as an alternative to organ transplantation.

Stem cell research offers a lot of potential for improving human health in the future. Much research is still needed to perfect the methods for differentiating stem cells in the lab, for making them function properly in the patient's body over a long time, and for reducing the chances of immune response rejection of the cells.

cancer. They can then make informed decisions about things they can do, such as surgery, to prevent getting the cancer.

Challenges for the Future

At the beginning of the twenty-first century, countless problems in human medicine have been solved. With the development of the germ theory, antisepsis, antibiotics, and greatly improved public health and sanitation measures, many infectious diseases such as plague, polio, and smallpox are no longer the deadly threats they once were. New ways to diagnose illnesses help find diseases sooner and treat them in their early stages. New techniques such as minimally invasive surgery and safe, effective anesthesia make surgery a safe treatment option for many health issues. New drugs are being developed every day to treat hundreds of human health conditions. People are living longer and healthier than at any time in history.

With improved health and longer life, however, comes a new set of issues. It is estimated that by 2050, the number of Americans over the age of sixty-five will reach 80 million. Living longer means more time to get sick, and illnesses associated with a long life, such as arthritis, heart disease, kidney disease, diabetes, and Alzheimer's dementia, are on the rise. Billions of dollars are spent each year on researching and treating the diseases of old age.

Another challenge for the future has arisen directly out of the use and overuse of antibiotics, the miracle drugs of the twentieth century. Bacteria have the ability to change their own genetics in response to their environment. In response to the ever-growing use of antibiotics, several kinds of bacteria have become genetically immune, or resistant, to antibiotics that were once effective against them. The best-known example is methicillin-resistant staphylococcus aureus, or MRSA. MRSA is an antibiotic-resistant form of a common skin bacterium. It first appeared in the 1960s and was most commonly seen in hospitalized patients. Since the 1980s, however, there has been a significant rise in community-based MRSA infec-

tions. It causes skin infections that can spread into the lungs or other parts of the body and, in severe cases, can lead to sepsis and death. MRSA and other antibiotic-resistant organisms have become a significant public health issue.

Two very significant medical challenges, particularly in the United States, are the health issues involved with tobacco use and the obesity epidemic that has arisen over the last decade. In the United States illnesses related to tobacco use account for almost 450,000 deaths each year and shorten the average life span by ten to twenty years. Tobacco use has been directly linked to illnesses such as high blood pressure, heart attacks, strokes, circulatory diseases, chronic obstructive lung disease, and many kinds of cancer. The major chemical in tobacco smoke, nicotine, is highly addictive, however, and it can be extremely difficult to quit smoking. Extensive public education campaigns, nicotine patches, and new drugs that change nicotine's effect in the brain have helped reduce tobacco use, but an average of 25 percent of Americans still smoke.

Illness related to obesity is second only to tobacco use in the number of deaths caused each year, at about three hundred thousand. Obesity is linked to illnesses such heart disease, high blood pressure, diabetes, respiratory problems, arthritis, and chronic back pain. Obesity is measured using the body mass index (BMI), a ratio of weight to height. A person with a BMI of over 30 is considered to be obese. During the

1990s the percentage of obese Americans rose from 12 to 18 percent. Several factors have contributed to this trend. Electronic technologies such as video games and television have contributed to a sharp decrease in physical activity, especially among children, who make up one of the fastest-growing groups of obese Americans. The fast-food industry, a product of the fast-paced American culture of convenience, has traditionally offered foods that are very high in fat and calories (although most fast-food chains are now offering healthier menu choices). Public education about nutrition, more physical education in schools, more parental involvement in the activities of children, and healthier food choices in schools, restaurants, and workplaces can all help to reverse this trend.

A final challenge for medicine in the future has to do with economics. Modern high-tech medical science carries with it extremely high costs for both patient and provider. According to British physician and geneticist David Weatherall:

> The current high-technology medical practice based on modern scientific medicine must steadily increase health expenditures. Regardless of the mechanisms for the provision of health care, its spiraling costs . . . combined with greater public awareness and demand for medical care, are resulting in a situation in which most industrial countries are finding it impossible to control the costs of providing health care services.[47]

As a result, some countries are struggling with the possibility of having to ration health-care services. In addition, high costs make modern health care less accessible to those in developing countries. The economics of health care is a major point of concern for the future of medicine.

Notes

Introduction: From Shaman to Surgeon

1. Quoted in Albert S. Lyons. "Prehistoric Medicine." Health Guidance—Free Health Articles, March 26, 2007. www.healthguidance.org/entry/6303 /1/Prehistoric-Medicine.html.

Chapter One: The Beginning: Primitive and Ancient Medicine

2. Quoted in Roy Porter. *The Greatest Benefit to Mankind: A Medical History of Humanity*. New York: Norton, 1997, p. 14.
3. Porter. *The Greatest Benefit to Mankind*, p. 18.
4. Quoted in Robert D. Biggs. "Medicine, Surgery, and Public Health in Ancient Mesopotamia." *Journal of Assyrian Academic Studies*, 2005, p. 4. www.jaas.org/edocs/v19n1/Biggs-Medicine,%20surgery.pdf.
5. Quoted in Biggs. "Medicine, Surgery, and Public Health in Ancient Mesopotamia," p. 16.
6. Quoted in Ryan Greiner. "Ancient Egyptian Medicine." Creighton University, December 11, 2001. http://puffin .creighton.edu/museums/greiner.
7. Quoted in Massoume Price. "History of Ancient Medicine in Mesopotamia and Iran." Iran Chamber Society, October, 2001. www.iranchamber.com /history/articles/ancient_medicine_ mesopotamia_iran.php.
8. Quoted in James Henry Breasted, ed. *The Edwin Smith Surgical Papyrus*. Chicago: University of Chicago Press, 1930, p. 140.
9. Quoted in Breasted. *The Edwin Smith Surgical Papyrus*, p. 312.
10. Maurice Bloomfield, trans. "Hymns of the Athar-Veda." Sacred Books of the East, vol. 42, Hymn II, 32. www .intratext.com/ixt/ENG0042/_P1S .HTM.
11. Chinmaya Yuva Kendra, comp. *Awakening Indians to India*. Mumbai: Central Chinmaya Mission Trust, 2008, p. 439.

Chapter Two: Greek and Roman Medicine

12. Theodor Alois Buckley, trans. *The Iliad of Homer*. London: Henry G. Bohn, 1851, p. 69.
13. Quoted in Porter. *The Greatest Benefit to Mankind*, p. 61.
14. Quoted in Porter. *The Greatest Benefit to Mankind*, p. 69.
15. Quoted in Porter. *The Greatest Benefit to Mankind*, p. 69.
16. Quoted in History Learning Site. "Medicine in Ancient Rome." www .historylearningsite.co.uk/medicine_ in_ancient_rome.htm.
17. Quoted in History Learning Site. "Medicine in Ancient Rome."

18. Porter. *The Greatest Benefit to Mankind*, p. 73.
19. Quoted in Porter. *The Greatest Benefit to Mankind*, p. 77.
20. Porter. *The Greatest Benefit to Mankind*, p. 82.
21. Porter. *The Greatest Benefit to Mankind*, p. 82.

Chapter Three: Medicine in the Middle Ages

22. Porter. *The Greatest Benefit to Mankind*, p. 84.
23. Quoted in Porter. *The Greatest Benefit to Mankind*, p. 88.
24. Quoted in Cecilia C. Mettler. *History of Medicine*. Philadelphia: Blakiston, 1947, p. 186.
25. Quoted in William Rosen. *Justinian's Flea—Plague, Empire, and the Birth of Europe*. New York. Viking, 2007, p. 223.

Chapter Four: Medical Awakening: The Renaissance

26. Porter. *The Greatest Benefit to Mankind*, p. 163.
27. Quoted in Francisco Guerra. "The Earliest American Epidemic: The Influenza of 1493." *Social Science History*, Autumn 1988, p. 309.
28. Quoted in Guerra. "The Earliest American Epidemic: The Influenza of 1493," p. 311.
29. Quoted in Porter. *The Greatest Benefit to Mankind*, p. 166.
30. Quoted in Mettler. *History of Medicine*, p. 37.
31. Quoted in Porter. *The Greatest Benefit to Mankind*, p. 186.
32. Quoted in Porter. *The Greatest Benefit to Mankind*, p. 187.

33. Quoted in Jennifer Viegas. "Renaissance Hospitals Resembled Spas." Discovery Channel, April 23, 2007. http://dsc.discovery.com/news/2007/04/23/hospitals_his.html?category=history&guid=20070423113000.
34. Quoted in Porter. *The Greatest Benefit to Mankind*, p. 202.
35. Quoted in Jolande Jacobi, ed. *Selected Writings: Paracelsus*. New York: Pantheon, 1951, pp. 79–80.

Chapter Five: Medical Revolution in the Age of Reason

36. Quoted in Porter. *The Greatest Benefit to Mankind*, p. 266.
37 Quoted in H.M. Plunkett. "Lady Mary Wortley Montagu and Modern Bacteriology." *Popular Science Monthly*, July 1894, p. 361.
38. Quoted in Porter. *The Greatest Benefit to Mankind*, p. 341.
39. Quoted in Amer Chaikuri. "The Magnificent Century of Cardiothoracic Surgery." *Heart Views*, March–May 2008. www.hmc.org.qa/heartviews/vol9no1/history_med1.htm.
40. Quoted in David M. Knipe and Peter M. Howley, eds. *Fields Virology*. 5th ed. Philadelphia: Lippincott Williams and Wilkins, 2007, p. 1365.
41. Quote in John Carey, ed. "Old Tyme Mastectomy." Eyewitness to History. http://wesclark.com/jw/mastectomy.html.

Chapter Six: Challenges in the Twentieth Century and Beyond

42. Quoted in Complete Dictionary of Scientific Biography. "Ehrlich, Paul."

Encyclopedia.com. www.encyclopedia
.com/topic/Paul_Ehrlic.aspx.

43. Quoted in Joseph Sambrook and David William Russell. *Molecular Cloning: A Laboratory Manual*. Vol. 2. Cold Spring Harbor, NY: Cold Spring Harbor Laboratory, 2001, p. 1153.

44. Quoted in Porter. *The Greatest Benefit to Mankind*, p. 614.

45. Quoted in John Quinlan. "Da Vinci Robot Brings Precision to Surgery." *Sioux City Journal.com*, May 19, 2011.

www.siouxcityjournal.com/lifestyl
es/health-med-fit/article_55da16bf
-5134-5473-b4c6-4a8d8a3c7f04.html.

46. Quoted in *Science Daily*. "Genetic Pathways Involved in Breast Cancer Identified." March 3, 2011. www
.sciencedaily.com/releases/2011/03
/110303120852.htm.

47. David Weatherall, et al. "Science and Technology for Disease Control: Past, Present, and Future." www
.ncbi.nlm.nih.gov/books/NBK117
40.

Glossary

acetum: A substance similar to vinegar used in ancient times to cleanse wounds.

aesclepia: An ancient Greek medical school.

alchemy: The ancient art of medical chemistry.

anatomy: The study of the physical structure of an organism.

anesthesia: The administration of drugs to cause unconsciousness during surgery.

animalcules: The name given by Antoni van Leeuwenhoek to the organisms he saw under his microscope.

antibiotics: A class of drugs used for treating and preventing infections.

antibodies: Protein molecules that can bind with foreign substances to make them harmless to the body.

antiseptic: A chemical that can kill germs on surfaces.

apothecary: A medieval term for a druggist or pharmacist.

asepsis: The concept of removing germs on surfaces or surgical instruments.

attenuate: To weaken a virus.

auscultation: A method of listening to the sounds made by the internal organs such as the heart and lungs.

ayurveda: The ancient Eastern holistic approach to maintaining health.

bacteria: Microscopic, one-celled organisms involved in many biological processes, including disease.

bloodletting: The outdated practice of restoring health by opening a vein and letting blood out.

dissection: The process of opening and examining the internal structure of an animal.

endemic: A disease that is always present in a particular area or population.

epidemic: An unusually widespread outbreak of a disease.

filterable virus: The early name given to filtered liquids that contained viral particles, before viruses had been discovered.

gene therapy: The use of altered genes to treat genetic diseases and conditions.

genetic engineering: The process of altering genetic material to change the characteristics of an organism or to produce a biological product such as insulin.

humors: The ancient Greek name for the four bodily fluids that must be in balance for good health.

immunity: The state of being unsusceptible or resistant to a disease.

infectious: A disease that can be transmitted between individuals.

inoculation: The process of introducing an organism into the body in order to stimulate the immune system to produce antibodies.

laparoscope: A long, thin lens used for examining the inside of the abdomen or pelvis.

metastasis: The spread of cancer cells from one part of the body to another.

miasma: The ancient term for "bad air," thought to cause disease.

microbe: A microscopic organism.

oncogenes: A gene that can cause cells to become cancerous.

pandemic: A widespread epidemic of a disease affecting several countries.

parasite: An organism that lives on another organism and causes it harm.

pasteurization: The process of killing germs in foods, especially dairy products.

pathogen: An organism that causes disease; a germ.

prognosis: A prediction of the probable outcome of a disease.

puerperal fever: An infection of the uterus following childbirth.

putrefaction: The decay of plant or animal remains.

sedative: A medication that causes relaxation or sleepiness.

sepsis: An infection in the blood that affects the entire body.

shaman: A primitive healer.

spontaneous generation: The outdated idea that organisms can arise from a nonliving substance.

stem cells: Cells that have not yet become specialized for any particular function.

trepanation: The ancient practice of opening the skull to release evil spirits.

vaccination: The name given by Edward Jenner to his method of inoculation.

virus: A nonliving particle of genetic material that can invade cells and cause disease.

For More Information

Books

James Cross Giblin. *When Plague Strikes: The Black Death, Smallpox, AIDS*. New York: Harper Collins, 1995. The story of three of the deadliest diseases in history.

Noah Gordon. *The Physician*. London: Little, Brown, 2001. In this work of historical fiction, an eleventh-century boy travels across Europe after his mother's death to the renowned medical school of the Persian physician Avicenna.

Louise Chipley Slavicek. *The Black Death*. New York: Chelsea House, 2008. The story of the thirteenth-century plague pandemic.

John Townsend. *Pox, Pus, and Plague: A History of Disease and Infection*. Chicago: Heinemann-Raintree, 2007. Part of the Painful History of Medicine series. A history of disease and infection through the ages.

Gareth Williams. *Angel of Death: The Story of Smallpox*. New York: St. Martin's, 2010. A history of smallpox from its beginnings to its eradication.

Lisa Yount. *The History of Medicine*. San Diego: Lucent, 2002. A comprehensive history of medicine from antiquity to the twentieth century.

Websites

Donate Life America (http://donatelife.net). An alliance of state and national organizations devoted to increasing organ and tissue donation.

History of Medicine, ABPI Resources for Schools (www.abpischools.org.uk/res/coResourceImport/resources04/history/index.cfm). A fun, interactive time line covering medical history from 8000 B.C. to the twenty-first century.

History of Medicine, Kidipede (www.historyforkids.org/learn/science/medicine/index.htm). A history of medicine with links to a multitude of topics in medical history.

History of Medicine, Kidswork! (www.knowitall.org/kidswork/hospital/history/index.html). A time line of medical history from ancient times to modern medicine.

Index

A

Acupuncture, 28
Adam and Eve, 14
Agricultural revolution, 16–17
AIDS (acquired immunodeficiency
 syndrome), 96–98
Alchemy, 75
Alcmaeon, 31
Alexander the Great, 34
Allison, S. Scott, 83
Anatomy, 31, 80
 contributions from Greek physicians,
 34
 Harvey and, 74
 Leonardo and, 68
 Renaissance advances in, 66–67, 75
Ancient Eastern medicine, 26–28
Ancient Greek medicine, 29–34
Ancient Roman medicine, 34–42
Andrechek, Eran, 104
Anesthesia, 90–91, 95
Antibiotics, 12
 bacterial resistance to, 106
Antibodies, 92–93
Antimony, 72
Antisepsis, 90
Antonine Plague (165 A.D.), 40, 41
Antoninus, Marcus Aurelius (Roman
 emperor), 40, 41
Apollo, 38
Apothecaries, 70–72, *71*
Aqueducts, *36*, 37
Aristotle, 32, 35, *35*
Asclepius (Greek deity), *30*, 30–31, 38
Ashipu (Mesopotamian healers), 21
Assyria, 21
Asu (Mesopotamian healers), 21–22
Atharva Veda, 26

B

Averroës (Ibn Rushd), 10, 53
Avicenna (Ibn Sina), 10, 52, *52*, 53
Ayurveda, 27, 28

Baillie, Matthew, 77, 78
Barnard, Christiaan, 100, *100*
Bichat, Marie Francois Xavier, 77
Black Death (Bubonic plague), 10, 12,
 50, 54–58
Block, Craig, 101
Blood, circulation of, 41, 67
Bloodletting, 22, 32–33, 42, 51, 65, 78
 Church's ban on, 47
Body mass index (BMI), 107
Bonaparte, Napoléon, 80
Buddhism, 26
Byzantine Empire, 42

C

Caesar Augustus, 34, 38–39
Cancer, 103–104
Canon of Medicine (Avicenna), 52
Carbolic acid (phenol), 90
Carrell, Alexis, 98–99
Casas, Bartolome de Las, 61–62
CAT (computerized tomography) scan,
 12, 20
Cato, 36
Cell theory, 77, 80–81
Celsus, 39
Centers for Disease Control and
 Prevention (CDC), 97
Cesarean section, 45, 47
Charaka, 26
Chi (flow of energy), 28
Chinese medicine, 28

Chloroform, 91
Christianity, medieval medicine and, 45, 47
Christianity/Christian church, Black Death and, 56
Cicero, Marcus Tullius, 36–37
Cocaine, 91
Cocoa, 71
Code of Hammurabi, 20, *21*, 30
Columbus, Bartholomew, 62
Columbus, Christopher, 61–62
Columella, Lucius Junius Moderatus, 37
Commodus (Roman emperor), 40
Computerized tomography (CAT) scan, 12, 20
Copernicus, Nicholas, 75
Coronary artery bypass grafts (CABG), 99
Cortés, Hernán, 63
Cushing, Harvey, 98

D
Davy, Humphrey, 90
De Humani Corporis Fabrica (Vesalius), 67, 75
De Motu Cordis (Harvey), 67
Deoxyribonucleic acid (DNA), 101, 104
  discovery of molecular structure of, 102
De sedibus et causis morborum (Morgagni), 77
Disease
  ancient explanations for, 14–15, 19, 25
  archeological evidence of, 20
  early Christian view of, 47
  Enlightenment and new understanding of, 77
  introduction into New World, 62
  linked to proximity to animals, 17, 19
  rise of agriculture and, 17
  spread of, 22
  theories on, 83–84
Djoser (pharaoh), 23
DNA. *See* Deoxyribonucleic acid
Domagk, Gerhard, 94
Donate Life America, 100

Drugs/medications
  antibiotic, 93–95, 106
  anticancer, 104
  Avicenna's contribution to, 52
  eighteenth century advancements in, 81
  for HIV illness, 98
  immunosuppressive, 100
  voyages of discovery and, 71–72
  See also specific drugs

E
Eastern medicine. *See* Ancient Eastern medicine
Ebers Papyrus, 24, 25–26
Edwin Smith Papyrus, 23, 25
Egyptian civilization, 22–26
Ehrlich, Paul, 92–94, *93*, 104
Enlightenment (age of reason), 76–80
  quackery during, 87
Epidemics
  emergence of, 17–19
  Roman view of, 37
Ether, 90–91

F
Fabiola, 47
Fleming, Alexander, 94–95
Fracastoro, Girolamo, 65, 83, 84
Francis, Thomas, 96

G
Galen, Claudius, 39–42, 47, 52, 53, 67
Galtier, Pierre, 86
Gama, Vasco da, 63
Genes, 101
Gene therapy, 103
Genetics, 101–103
Germ theory, 83, 90, 96
  Koch's work in, 87–88
Global Eradication Initiative, 96
Graham, James, 87
Gray's Anatomy, 80
Great Cannon of Medicine (Yellow Emperor of China). *See Inner Canon of the Yellow Emperor*

Greek medicine. *See* Ancient Greek medicine
Gregory VII (pope), 54
Guiaic, 71

H
Halle, John, 69
Hammurabi, 20
Harvey, William, 67, 74
Henderson, John, 70
Herodotus, 33
High Middle Ages, 54
Hinduism, 26
Hippocrates, 31–34, *32*, 47, 52, 76
  Galen on, 41
  on training of surgeons, 69
  translation into Arabic, 53
Hippocratic Corpus, 31, 34
The Histories (Herodotus), 33
History of the Peloponnesian Wars (Thucydides), 33
HIV (human immunodeficiency virus), 97, *97*
Homer, 25, 30
Hooke, Robert, 74
Hospitals, 39
  Byzantine, *48*, 49
  during High Middle Ages, 54
  Islamic, 53
  Protestant Reformation and, 66, 69
Human Genome Project, 103
Human papillomavirus (HPV), 104
Humoral theory, 32–33, 42, 56, 65
  Paracelsus and, 74

I
Ibn Rushd. *See* Averroës
Ibn Sina. *See* Avicenna
Imhotep, 23
Immunity, 92–93
Industrial Revolution, 11
Influenza, 17, 96
Inner Canon of the Yellow Emperor (Yu Hsing), 12, 28
Islamic medicine, 51–54
Islamic world, 10

J
Janssen, Hans, 74
Janssen, Zacharias, 74
Jenner, Edward, *79*, 80
Jerome (saint), 47
John of Ephesus, 49
Julius Caesar, 34
Justinian (Byzantine emperor), 47

K
Kergaradec, Jean Alexandre Le Jumeau de, 82
Knights Templar, 54
Koch, Robert, 84, 87, *88*, 89
Koch's postulates, 89

L
Laënnec, René-Théophile-Hyacinthe, 81–82
Laparoscopic surgery, 99, 101
Largus, Scribonius, 39
Laudanum, 74
Leeuwenhoek, Antoni van, 74, 83
Leonardo da Vinci, 11, 66, 67, 68, *68*
Life expectancy, 12
  increase in, 106
Lister, Joseph, 89–90
Long, Crawford, 90
Luther, Martin, 65

M
Macewan, William, 98
Magellan, Ferdinand, 63
Magnetic resonance imaging (MRI), 12
Malpighi, Marcello, 74
Margarita Philosophica (Reisch), 11
Mather, Increase, 62
Medical protestants, 72
Medications. *See* Drugs/medications
Mendel, Gregor, 102, *102*
Mental illness, in Middle Ages, 50
Mercury, 62, 72
Mesopotamia, 19
  cultures of, 20–21
Metchnikoff, Ilya, 92
Methicillin-resistant staphylococcus

aureus (MRSA), 106
Microscope, 74
Midwives, medieval, 46
Montagu, Mary Wortley, 78, 80
Morgagni, Giovanni Battista, 77, *77*
Morris, Robert, 81
MRI (magnetic resonance imaging), 12
MRSA (methicillin-resistant staphylococcus aureus), 106

N
Neolithic period (10,000 B.C. to 7000 B.C.), primitive treatments of, 15–16
New World, impact of Europeans' arrival in, 61–64
Nightingale, Florence, 83
Nurses, medieval, 46
Nurses/nursing, Renaissance, 70

O
Obesity, 106–107
The Odyssey (Homer), 25
Opium, 72
Organ transplantation, 100
Oribasius (Byzantine physician), 47, 49

P
Paget, Stephen, 98
Paleopathology, 20
Pandora, 14, *15*
Paracelsus (Theophrastus Philippus Aureolus Bombastus von Hohenheim), 72, *73*, 74–75
Paré, Ambroise, 69
Pasteur, Louis, 84, *85*, 86
Patent medicines, 87
Pathology, 77
Paul of Aegina, 49
Penicillin, 94–95
Pharmacy science, 70–72, 81
Phipps, James, 80
Pizarro, Francisco, 63
Plague of Athens (430 B.C.), 33, 41
Plague of Justinian (542), 49–51
Ponce de León, Juan, 63

Porter, Roy, 17, 39, 42, 61
Protestant Reformation, 65–66, 72
Public health, 11
  in ancient Rome, 37
  during High Middle Ages, 54
Puerperal fever (sepsis after childbirth), 89

Q
Quinine, 71

R
Rabies, 84, 86
Razi (Rhazes), 10, 53
Reisch, Gregor, 11
Renaissance, 11, 58, 59, 61
  hospitals in, 69–70
  pharmacy science in, 70–72
  Protestant Reformation and, 65–66
Roman medicine. *See* Ancient Roman medicine
Röntgen, Wilhelm, 81
Ruffer, Marc Armand, 20
Rush, Benjamin, 78

S
Salvarsan, 94
Schleiden, Matthias, 77, 80
Schwann, Theodor, 77, 80
Semmelweis, Ignaz, 89
Seven Books of Medicine (Paul of Aegina), 49
Shamans (religious healers), 19
Sixtus IV (pope), 66
Smallpox, 17, 40
  arrival in New World, 62
  eradication of, 96
  inoculation against, 78, *79*, 80
  vaccination against, 80
Sodium pentothal, 95
Sphygmomanometer, 81
Spirometer, 81
Spontaneous generation, 84
Stanley, Wendell, 96
Stem cell therapy, 105
Step pyramid (Saqqara), *23*

Stethoscope, 11, 81–83, *82*
Sulfa drugs, 94
Sumerian civilization, 20
Superstition, in Byzantine medicine, 49
Surgery
  development of anesthesia for, 90–91
  early Christian ban on, 45, 47
  Islamic advances in, 53
  medical advances revolutionizing, 11
  minimally invasive, 99, 101
  prehistoric, 15–16, *16*
  pre-Renaissance, 67, 69
  Renaissance advances in, 69
  robotic, 101
  sepsis and, 89–90
  in twentieth century, 98–99
  war and advances in, 39
Sushruta, 28
Syphilis, 62
  first antibiotics for, 93–94
  treatment for, 71, 72

T
Taijitu, 27, *27*
Theriacs, 72
Thermometer, 81
Thucydides, 33, 41
Tobacco, 71
  illnesses linked to, 106
  linked to cancer, 104
Tonsillectomy, 98
Trepanation, 15–16, *16*
Twelve Books of Medicine (Alexander of Tralles), 49
Twenty-first century, medical challenges of, 12–13

U
UNAIDS, 98
Universities, 54

V
Vaccines/vaccination, 80
  anticancer, 104
  for influenza, 96
  Pasteur and, 84
Varro, Marcus Terentius, 37
Vesalius, Andreas, 11, 66–67, 75
Victoria (English queen), 91
Virchow, Rudolf, 80–81
Viruses, 95–96
  role in cancer, 104
Vitruvian Man (Leonardo da Vinci), 68

W
War
  advances in surgery and, 69
  Roman medical advances and, 38–39
Weatherall, David, 107
WHO (World Health Organization), 96
Women, in medieval medicine, 46
World Health Organization (WHO), 96

X
X-rays, 81

Y
Yellow Emperor of China, 12
Yersina pestis, 49
Yin yang, 27
Yu Hsing (Chinese emperor), 28

Z
Zinke, Georg Gottfried, 86

Picture Credits

About the Author

Lizabeth Hardman received her bachelor of science degree in nursing from the University of Florida in 1978 and her bachelor of science degree in education from Southwest Missouri State University in 1991. She currently works full-time as a surgical nurse. She has two daughters, Rebecca and Wendy, and lives in Springfield, Missouri, with two dogs and two cats.